LEGENDARY

TIGER STADIUM

The Golden Band from Tigerland energizes LSU fans before a contest. (AP Photo)

LEGENDARY

TIGER STADIUM

THE 30 GREATEST LSU FOOTBALL GAMES

CHET HILBURN

PELICAN PUBLISHING COMPANY

GRETNA 2013

*The word "Pelican" and the depiction of a pelican are
trademarks of Pelican Publishing Company, Inc., and are
registered in the U.S. Patent and Trademark Office.*

Library of Congress Cataloging-in-Publication Data

Hilburn, Chet.
  Legendary Tiger stadium: the thirty greatest LSU football games / Chet
Hilburn.
       pages cm.
  ISBN 978-1-4556-1885-9 (pb : alk. paper) -- ISBN 978-1-4556-1886-6
(e-book) 1. Louisiana State University (Baton Rouge, La.)--Football--History.
2. LSU Tigers (Football team)--History. I. Title.
  GV958.L65H55 2013
  796.332'630976318--dc23
                               2013033093

*Front-cover photograph: LSU players display boot trophy after
   defeating Arkansas in 2011.* (AP Photo)

Printed in the United States of America

Published by Pelican Publishing Company, Inc.
1000 Burmaster Street, Gretna, Louisiana 70053

*To LSU Tiger fans everywhere, some of the most passionate
in all of college football*

CONTENTS

PREFACE

For LSU fans, Tiger Stadium at night is a place of wonderment, electricity, thrills, chills, sharpened senses, high drama, and a glorious feeling of oneness on a grand stage. It's a place where a person connects to a team and with the tens of thousands of others who occupy the same space. It's a stadium where a fan's dream can be fulfilled for a moment in time—an escape from the pressures, rigors, and doldrums of life. It's a venue where, for a brief while, success is not measured by one's life experiences but by what's happening on the field.

Emotions run high when the band marches out, the players run onto the field, or a Tiger tailback breaks into the open. LSU fans have always thought of themselves as part of the team itself and united with the thousands of other spectators through the creation of a single energy. The sum of the parts becomes the whole in Tiger Stadium, and the self is transported into another dimension—a place of magic, suspense, keen awareness, and most of all community. This is what sets Tiger Stadium apart from any other venue. Maybe this is why many longtime fans experience it as a holy place, something that becomes a cathedral on Saturday nights—a little piece of heaven.

Fans cheer during the first half of the LSU-West Virginia game in 2010. (AP Photo)

ACKNOWLEDGMENTS

I would like to give my heartfelt thanks to my brother, Wiley Hilburn, Jr., former head of the Louisiana Tech University Journalism Department and current columnist, for making me a diehard LSU football fan in 1961, when I was sixteen years old. I will always be grateful to him for having me down for Tiger games while he was working on his master's degree at the university. That was the beginning of my decades-long love affair with LSU football and Tiger Stadium.

Sincere thanks also go out to Patrick Spicer of Houston, whose keen eye caught some grammatical mistakes in the original text. I am also thankful for the various statistical Web sites that made my research so much easier. LSU football writers coming before me provided a great deal of essential background information. They are Peter Finney of the *New Orleans Times-Picayune*; Bud Johnson, former LSU Sports Information director; Marty Mulé, former writer for the *New Orleans Times-Picayune* and current LSU football author; and James Varney, of the *New Orleans Times-Picayune*.

LSU coach Les Miles gets players fired up and ready to take the field. (AP Photo/Gerald Herbert)

CHAPTER ONE

THE MAGIC OF TIGER STADIUM

Throughout the decades, since 1958, Louisiana State's Tiger Stadium has earned legendary status among college football stadiums in America. That reputation is hard to dispute. In the 1980s, Joanne Korth of the *St. Petersburg Times* wrote, "Fanaticism has made LSU's Tiger Stadium one of the most mystical venues" in all of college football. Georgia Tech coach Bobby Dodd declared in 1961 after departing with a 10-0 loss, "It was like the Roman Colosseum and we were the Christians." An ESPN survey of college football coaches in October 2007 picked Tiger Stadium as "by far the scariest place to play." Others have said it is more frenetic than the German Nuremberg rallies of the 1930s. One sportswriter called it an entity unto itself.

Whatever label a fan wants to place on LSU's Tiger Stadium, the electric atmosphere that Bayou Bengal fans produce on Saturday nights cannot be denied. The *Fort Worth Star Telegram* decades ago described the noise as similar to a jet-engine takeoff and louder than a rock concert.

Magazine writers have also pointed out how Tiger Stadium is in a class of its own. In 1989, *Sporting News* ranked it as the number-one place to attend a football game, and *Sport Magazine* in 1998 said it was the toughest place for an opponent to play. Gannett News Services called it the most dreaded road site in college football.

Former Kentucky coach Bill Curry said the noise in Tiger Stadium was unlike anything he had heard in his life and there was no place like it. Erin Andrews, formerly of ESPN, said no other campus could possibly bring the magic to a night game like Death Valley. Verne Lundquist of CBS said the 2007 LSU-Florida game was the loudest contest he had ever heard in decades of broadcasting college football, and he called it "an incredible atmosphere."

The stadium at night has long been known as a house of horrors for opposing players and visitors alike—a venue where darkness rules. The black sky is not a good omen for visitors. As the late ESPN commentator Beano Cook once said, "Dracula and LSU are at their best when the sun goes down." No one would argue with that.

CBSsports.com writer Dennis Dodd said of the stadium in 2009:

It has turned the knees of Americans to goo. It has caused coaches to lose their coaching minds. It only happens at a special space at a special time. LSU can be up, LSU can be down, but LSU's best weapon remains sunset. Dark.

That combined with Tiger Stadium on a Saturday night is something loud, strange and holy. There is noise in stadiums everywhere from Eugene to Tuscaloosa. Only in Baton Rouge is there a living, breathing being lurking in its grand, old stadium.

Perhaps the spell is cast at night to bedevil opponents. Author and former Tiger center John Ed Bradley believes that the stadium is haunted and "all the ghosts are on LSU's side."

Adding to the mystique of the venue are the giant magnolia trees and the abandoned dormitory rooms that loom across the exterior of the mammoth structure, providing the magical atmosphere of a bygone era. Stir 150,000 fans into the scene, some juiced, and you have a boiling pot of witch's brew.

Whether one thinks that Tiger Stadium holds a devilish grip over its opponents or that the Tigers have superior talent, the fact remains that LSU has lost only four contests at night in its stadium since 2002.

The most likely reason for all the mystique surrounding the venue is the packed stadium itself. Rising from its dark, tunneled recesses below to a thunderous spectacle above, it comes alive on Saturdays through unrelenting crowd energy that gives the nearly century-old edifice its life and personality. Perhaps this is when the venue becomes an entity unto itself. There's no doubt that games at night are not a welcome sight for opponents entering the den of salivating Tigers and fans.

The stadium and crowd hysteria have long been a symbol of radical unity among LSU fans. Louisianans and others across the nation have succumbed to the mystique of Death Valley, where the thunderous noise stays within the confines of the stadium. During one legendary game, the fans released energy powerful enough to record an earthquake in Baton Rouge.

Erin Andrews, formerly of ESPN, loved night games at Tiger Stadium. (AP Photo/Tom DiPace)

Some followers call their passion for LSU football "worship," and indeed it is for many fans. Larry Aycock, owner of a preschool in Lafayette, Louisiana, and one of the most ardent Tiger fans, calls it a "cathedral in a stadium." He continues, "It's so special . . . it's actually worship. You never schedule a family wedding when LSU is playing in Tiger Stadium."

As darkness settles in for night games, the scene turns chaotic around 6:50 as LSU players run onto the field to a thunderous roar. Whiskey is taken out of concealed areas in clothing, women's purses, and binoculars doubling as flasks. Tension builds until kickoff around 7:08—the time when legends are born in Tiger Stadium.

Indeed, legend was created on Halloween night in 1959 by one of the most electrifying runs in college football. Heisman Trophy winner Billy Cannon practically ran over an entire Ole Miss team for a winning touchdown. The titanic defensive struggle allowed LSU to triumph in a brutally fought 7-3 contest.

A grainy black-and-white film of the run still marks Halloween night for many football fans across the nation. In a surreal atmosphere of darkness and fog, Cannon thundered into

Billy Cannon helped LSU go undefeated in 1958. (AP Photo)

football immortality in an eighty-nine-yard run with a determination seldom seen on a football field. Another legend, All-American Rebel quarterback and punter Jake Gibbs—the last man between Cannon and the end zone—barely missed a tackle that could have erased the significance of the Halloween run. But that was not the case, and the play is forever etched in the minds of LSU football fans.

Throughout the years, Tiger Stadium has earned a reputation as one of the most intimidating sports facilities anywhere. An article by football writer Tim Yu listed it as the third most inhospitable place to play in the world. Only soccer stadiums La Bombonera in Buenos Aires, Argentina, and Ali Sami Yen Stadium in Istanbul, Turkey, topped Tiger Stadium. More significantly, it is the only American college football venue to make the list. Only two other U.S. stadiums did—the Green Bay Packers' Lambeau Field at number nine, followed by the old Yankee Stadium in New York at number ten.

Kent DeJean, a Baton Rouge attorney, LSU graduate, and avid Tiger fan known to Internet users as "The Evil Twin," describes Tiger Stadium as "magical, not like anything I have ever experienced." He adds, "It's intimidating and colorful . . . it reminds me of a European soccer match. The crowd seems to think it's a part of the game . . . the noise never ceases."

Kent DeJean claims that LSU fans have always been innovative about sneaking liquor into Tiger Stadium, although it is banned by the university. "People put it into their boots, strap it onto their backs . . . there's always a way to get it in if you want to badly enough," he says. "A few years ago several people strapped twenty whiskey flasks below the stadium seats before a game. Our culture is French-Catholic, and having fun drinking and enjoying life is part of our routine. Many years ago the life expectancy of a Louisiana Cajun was thirty-five years, and some of us have taken sort of a fatalistic attitude about life."

Scott, "Evil Twin Two" and a veterinarian practicing in Lafayette, Louisiana, remembers being mesmerized by the crowd when he first entered Tiger Stadium as a child with his

Kent DeJean, aka Evil Twin One (left), and his twin brother Scott, aka Evil Twin Two, are outspoken and rabid LSU fans who sit in the south end zone of the stadium. (Kent DeJean)

parents and brother. "Every Saturday in the fall that little kid inside me is reborn when my ticket is torn to enter the magical place again," he says. Sitting in the south end zone for many years, the brothers have played a unique role in the LSU stadium atmosphere, with their outspoken opinions and open questions to LSU coaches about anything and everything concerning Bayou Bengal sports.

The late Don Long of Lafayette, Louisiana, writer of an Internet column called *Dandy Don's LSU Recruiting News*, said about Tiger Stadium, "Early in the morning the tailgating begins. Raising as much hell as you are allowed to do and still remain on the grounds is the norm. I don't believe there is an atmosphere anywhere in the country to match it."

Wright Thompson of ESPN.com wrote in 2008, "It was electric. When Death Valley is rocking, it seems as if it might actually take flight. On Saturday, I went back to Baton Rouge to see Alabama barely beat LSU and was, once again, reminded that Tiger Stadium is the best place in the world to watch a sporting event."

In another twist to the experience, as many as fifty thousand fans never enter the venue. Instead, they party outside near their cars and campers, adding a surreal scene to the stadium grounds where bourbon flows throughout the night. "People are in awe of the stadium, but many choose just to party outside. Really, the whole thing is just one big party. I grew up with it and will die with it," said LSU graduate Jacques Duplantis of Houston.

Over the years, extraordinary games and plays have earned Tiger Stadium a unique reputation. In a 1988 game against Auburn, an earthquake registered in Baton Rouge when fans erupted into a frenzy following a game-winning ten-yard touchdown pass by quarterback Tommy Hodson to

A Tiger fan points toward the Gators before the start of a game in 2009. (AP Photo)

running back Eddie Fuller as time was running out. In 1972, "time stood still" when the "Ruston Rifle," quarterback Bert Jones, lofted a touchdown pass to running back Brad Davis with 00:01 left on the clock. The play won the game for the Tigers, to the dismay of the Ole Miss fans. In 2007, LSU graduate Pat Stuckey was sitting in the south end zone in a game against Florida. The Tigers converted five fourth-down plays and stung Florida and Tim Tebow in the last seconds for a rousing 28-24 win. "I was trembling and goose bumps were popping out," Stuckey recalls. "My flask of Jack Daniel's was emptied. The whole stadium went nuts."

In 1958, John F. Prejean from Jennings, Louisiana, was working on his master's degree at LSU. He recalled:

> Coming from a small town I couldn't believe it . . . when the Tigers took the field it was like the gladiators were coming out. The noise could actually hurt you. I thought many times of bringing ear plugs to the games but then the excitement would have not been the same. It was like being on a movie set that year . . . everybody was caught up as spectators in a year LSU went undefeated. A lot of kids neglected their studies at LSU that year and flunked out of school. All anyone thought about in 1958 was football.

An anonymous opposing fan summed up Tiger Stadium on an Internet sports blog when he wrote, "As for my own experience, if you've never been there, you'll never understand. And if you've been there, you will never be able to explain it. The only thing that could be better there would be an Aggie victory and just a little purple rain on a wet Tiger parade."

LSU fans get fired up before the start of the 2011 Arkansas game. (AP Photo)

Former athletic director Joe Dean decades ago said that LSU should build a new, modern, 100,000-seat stadium with up-to-date facilities. Tiger fans loudly booed the suggestion, and the fabled tradition continues at Tiger Stadium—one of the most colorful and feared, if not the most ancient, venues in the entire world.

LSU cheerleaders rally outside Tiger Stadium in 2011. (AP Photo/Gerald Herbert)

CHAPTER TWO

THE THIRTY GREATEST GAMES

Since 1958, when LSU won its first national championship, many great games have been played in Tiger Stadium before some of the most raucous fans in the world. Although opinions may vary as to the best contests played there, these thirty games are close to the author's heart and viewed by fans as unforgettable clashes in one of the greatest sports venues on the planet.

Billy Cannon runs through Ole Miss in 1959 for an eighty-nine-yard touchdown. (AP Photo)

NUMBER 1: THE GREATEST GAME
LSU 7, OLE MISS 3: OCTOBER 31, 1959

On Halloween night of 1959, the legend of Tiger Stadium was born. It was a very dark night, with humidity near 100 percent producing a mist as the eight o'clock kickoff approached. The field looked like a strange apparition under the lights, and fans could feel electricity in the air on the warm and muggy evening. Thus, on a night when the ghosts and goblins were out, the scene was set for one of the greatest games in college football.

LSU was the defending national champion and ranked number one by the Associated Press, but undefeated, number-three Mississippi sported legends of its own: Jack Gibbs, an option quarterback who had starred for many years as catcher for the New York Yankees; Head Coach Johnny Vaught, who would have rather played field position with his great defense and kicked on any down; and All-American fullback Charlie Flowers, who could run through a brick wall, dragging would-be tacklers along the way. Vaught died in 2006 at age ninety-six but will always be remembered for compiling a remarkable record of 190-61-12 for the Rebels. He would go down as one of college football's greatest coaches.

The first half of the game was like a version of *Nightmare on Elm Street* for LSU, as the Tigers fumbled three times. When tailback Billy Cannon fumbled at his twenty-yard line, fans were becoming restless. Would LSU's eighteen-game winning streak come to an end in Tiger Stadium against the hated Ole Miss Rebels?

It would be left up to the Tigers' defense as the Rebels were soon knocking on the door at the LSU three-yard line. On third down, Mississippi's scrambling quarterback Gibbs ran

LSU head coach Paul Dietzel congratulates Mickey Mangham in 1960. Mangham's stop of Gibbs near the Tiger end zone preserved a huge win over Ole Miss in 1959. (AP Photo)

right on a quarterback sweep but was hauled down by LSU defensive end Mickey Mangham for a loss at the five-yard line. Tiger fans loudly celebrated and breathed a little easier, although Ole Miss made a field goal to take a 3-0 lead at halftime.

Entering the third quarter, Ole Miss began to play ultra-conservatively, believing that LSU would not score against one of the greatest defenses to ever suit up for college football. Vaught had Gibbs punt on first down three consecutive times, hoping his punishing defense would give the Rebels the ball deep in Tiger territory on a wet field. Everything seemed hopeless for the Tigers after LSU head coach Paul Dietzel called for Cannon to fake a punt on fourth and nine from the Rebel thirty-five. Cannon was tackled for a one-yard loss.

However, the scene was set for the historic run a few plays later when Gibbs punted from his forty-two early in the fourth quarter. Cannon fielded the kick on a high bounce at his eleven-yard line. The rest is chronicled in college football lore. Cannon's dramatic run is still replayed across the state of Louisiana and by some national television stations on Halloween night. Other fans routinely watch it over the Internet.

Hugh McManus, a 1957 Ole Miss graduate and a resident of Houston, was sitting in the stands that night. He recalled:

> We were on the LSU side. The stadium was overflowing and loud. Gibbs' punting had put LSU in a hole all night, and Vaught figured he would win the game with his defense. Cannon took Gibbs' punt on about the eleven-yard line. It was the most incredible thing I have ever seen. He nearly ran over the entire Ole Miss team. People were standing, screaming, and hollering. The roar was deafening for about five minutes after the run.

Another spectator that night was teenager Wayne Schneider, also of Houston, who would later live the engaging life of both fan and student inside the dorm rooms of the huge stadium. Sitting in the upper deck of the south end zone, the LSU graduate said he had a great view of the run. "The place went crazy . . . it was bedlam," he stated, recalling that he put away a pint of whiskey during the game.

Cannon's run was no feat of brilliant jukes or quick moves. Instead, the 9.4 100-yard sprinter put his power and speed to the ultimate test. Either the Heisman Trophy winner ran over seven Ole Miss defenders or they bounced off him as he fought his way with brute strength along the Rebel sideline to college football glory.

Tiger fans loudly celebrated the run, but the game was not over. Tension continued to mount as Mississippi went on a late drive from its thirty-two, staying on the ground with the superb running of super sub Doug Elmore from his quarterback position.

Dietzel had brought a new concept to college

Wayne Schneider of Houston witnessed Cannon's run in 1959 and said the crowd went berserk when the tailback scored the touchdown. (Diane Daech)

football in 1958, using a three-platoon system that would give players adequate rest. All three teams could play on offense or defense, although the Go Team was primarily an offensive team. The Chinese Bandits stood out for defense but could also shift to offense. The White Team mainly consisted of the team's best athletes, who played both ways. In this game, Dietzel stuck with his famed defensive unit, the Chinese Bandits, until the Rebels reached the LSU twenty-three, where he substituted the exhausted bunch with the White Team.

Ninety seconds remained in the game when Elmore made a first down at the LSU seven-yard line. Three more running plays brought Ole Miss near the Tiger end zone. At fourth and goal, Elmore ran over the left tackle but was stopped inches from a touchdown by Cannon, doubling as a linebacker, and quarterback Warren Rabb, also playing double duty.

And suddenly, the legend of Tiger Stadium was born as the crowd went berserk and LSU ran out the clock for a 7-3 win. A special edition of *Sports Illustrated* recounted the most unforgettable college football games that its sportswriters covered over the decades. The LSU-Mississippi contest of 1959 led off the issue. Also in the front of the edition was a two-page color photo of the 2010 Tiger team and coaches, roaring their lungs out after a 43-36 victory over Ole Miss.

Overshadowed by Cannon's run is just how great the Ole Miss team was in 1959. Had it not been for his almost superhuman feat, Mississippi might have gone down as one of the best teams in college football, with an undefeated record and a whopping 350-14 scoring edge over opponents. Ole Miss outgained the Tigers in rushing yards 160-142, with LSU getting 29 yards in the air to 19 for the Rebels. Cannon rushed twelve times for 48 yards, and Flowers 35 yards on ten carries. Despite the loss, at least one Web site, *Football Outsiders,* has crowned the 1959 Rebels as the greatest team in college football.

Some of the Rebels still feel the sting of defeat from that night. Richard Price, an offensive lineman on the team, said at a reunion that he thinks about Cannon's run day and night. A nightmare, he suggests, is waking up and thinking it didn't happen for a moment—until reality sets in.

It's almost an afterthought that the Rebels defeated LSU in the Sugar Bowl in New Orleans that same season, 21-0. The same cannot be said of Cannon's astonishing feat in the regular-season game.

In the Sugar Bowl contest, in which LSU players first voted not to participate, the Tigers had a long list of injuries. In the backfield were Rabb with a strained knee, Johnny Robinson with a fractured hand, and halfback Wendell Harris with a broken leg. A wounded Rabb would not be an effective passer, as the Rebel defense successfully crowded the line of scrimmage to stop Cannon before he could get going. The offensive statistics were overwhelmingly in favor of the Rebels, with Ole Miss gaining 364 yards and the Tigers losing 15. Holding on for much of the first half, LSU's dominating defense became fatigued as time wore on. Right before the half, Ole Miss scored on a long touchdown pass. They registered two more touchdowns in the second half. With an ineffective and one-dimensional offense, the Tiger defense finally ran out of energy, having been on the field too long.

It was one of the first football games to be telecast coast to coast in color. Legend has it that tickets were paid for with refrigerator repairs, a used Cadillac, and a fourteen-foot fiberglass boat.

LSU would end the regular season ranked number three in the nation behind Syracuse and Ole Miss. It only stumbled against Tennessee in Knoxville, 14-13. With 334 total yards to 112 for the Vols, the Tigers dominated every aspect of the game except for the scoreboard. They had nineteen first downs to only nine for the Volunteers, as Cannon rushed for 122 yards and

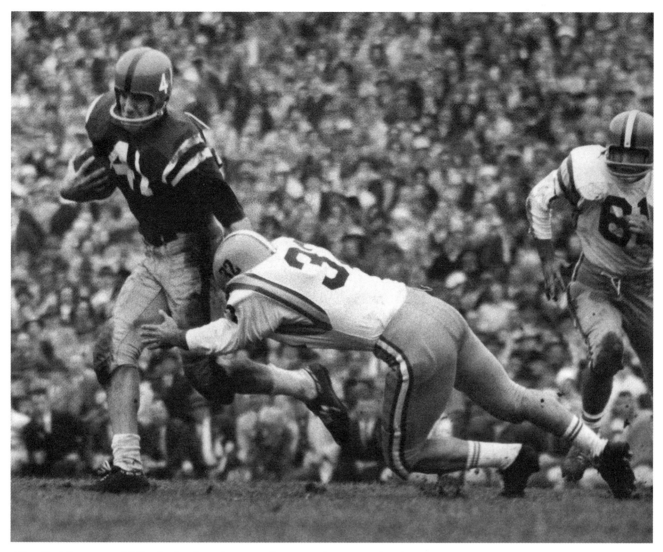

Charlie Flowers of Mississippi makes yardage against LSU in the 1960 Sugar Bowl. (AP Photo)

Robinson for 115. However, two fumbles and two interceptions were too much for the Tigers to overcome. Cannon's attempt at a 2-point conversion near the end of the contest failed, ending LSU's nineteen-game winning streak.

A win over Tennessee might have secured a second straight national championship for the Tigers, but it was not to be. An undefeated LSU team probably would not have played Ole Miss twice in a season, with the Rebels dropping in the rankings following the game. But in college football, nothing is a given. The Tigers had to play Alabama again in the 2012 season after defeating the Tide on its home field in November.

Underneath the goalposts after the Sugar Bowl, Cannon would sign a $100,000 contract with the Houston Oilers' Bud Adams, a big sum in those days. It was reported that Cannon also received a car and several service stations. Adams is still the owner of the team, now the Tennessee Titans.

NUMBER 2: THE HEARTBREAK GAME
USC 17, LSU 12: SEPTEMBER 29, 1979

In perhaps the hardest-fought game by LSU in Tiger Stadium, the Bayou Bengals came up short against the number-one team in the nation with a score of 17-12. Outmanned at nearly every position by a superior Southern California team boasting twelve All-Americans, the Tigers fought and clawed at the line of scrimmage and nearly pulled off the upset of the decade before a crazed crowd of 78,322 fans who never sat down or gave up. Called the "most talented team to ever play in Tiger Stadium" by outgoing LSU head coach Charles McClendon, the gifted Trojans were led by quarterback great Paul McDonald, Heisman Trophy winners Charles White and Marcus Allen, Lombardi Award winner Brad Budde, and future pro Hall of Famers Ronnie Lott in the secondary and Anthony Munoz on the offensive line.

No slouches themselves, especially on defense, the Tigers were led by never-say-die All-SEC defensive tackle Benjy Thibodeaux, All-SEC defensive ends John Adams and Lyman White, All-SEC nose guard George Atiyeh, All-SEC defensive backs Willie Teal and Chris Williams, All-SEC receiver Carlos Carson, and All-SEC offensive center John Ed Bradley.

At the end of the first half, Tiger fans were jubilant as LSU held a 9-3 lead, stuffing the Trojans' high-octane offense. Steve Ensminger had thrown a touchdown pass to LeRoid Jones, and Don Barthels had kicked a field goal for the 6-point lead. The extra point was missed, but LSU fans were nonetheless feeling pretty good.

Following another field goal, the Tigers clung to a 12-10 lead late in the fourth quarter on willpower alone. Then LSU got a huge break when USC tailback Allen fumbled on his twenty-two and Tiger nose guard Atiyeh recovered. But in a costly offensive series, the Bayou Bengals failed to take advantage of the miscue. They received a fifteen-yard penalty for offensive interference on their first play and then suffered a quarterback loss for two yards, a delay-of-game penalty, and another quarterback loss for six yards.

Taking over with a little more than three minutes remaining in the game, USC finally came alive. McDonald drove the Trojans relentlessly downfield and found speedy flanker Kevin Williams

Former LSU defensive tackle Benjy Thibodeaux said the tremendous stadium noise against USC in 1979 fired up the Tigers. (Paige Penland)

Charles McClendon had his team ready to play top-ranked USC in 1979. (AP Photo)

open in the end zone for a touchdown that won the game with thirty-two seconds left. LSU's depleted but courageous defense had finally caved in. A last-second pass from LSU's Ensminger went through the hands of speedster Willie Turner in the Trojan end zone, much to the dismay of the Tiger fans.

LSU fans in attendance that night still believe that game officials may have allowed USC to win the contest by not catching the movement of a Southern Cal offensive lineman before the snap on the winning drive. Instead, a Pacific Ten official threw a questionable flag against a hard-charging Thibodeaux for touching the facemask of quarterback McDonald. The call gave the Trojans a first down on the winning drive.

Recalling the game decades later, Thibodeaux said, "The roar that night was so loud and continuous, it permeated through our body fibers. It infused us with the belief that we would prevail against the odds. No other game in Tiger Stadium in which I played produced that much noise."

The former defensive tackle remembers the contest as bittersweet, because although victory slipped away, most fans remember him from that game. The former LSU defensive standout said, "My life has been enriched by the USC game, and it will always carry a special place in my heart." Certainly, character and toughness were built into every Tiger on the field that evening.

Author John Ed Bradley, center for the Tigers on the 1979 team, wrote in a *Sports Illustrated* article that McClendon, on his deathbed, had asked him if he ever thought back to the USC game. "I remember it all the time," Bradley, captain of the Tiger team, told him. "I don't want to remember it because we lost, Coach, but I remember it."

Bradley also remembers the roar of the crowd. "The noise level is always a factor in Tiger Stadium, but that night it exceeded anything I'd ever heard," he said. "It sounded like a physical force . . . everything was just a howl." In fact, the crowd was so loud that evening

Lott will never forget his experience with LSU fans in 1979. (AP Photo/Greg Trott)

that LSU Radio Network announcers John Ferguson and Walter Hill had a tough time being heard on the air. Trojan Budde said after the game that the crowd hysteria in Tiger Stadium that night made Notre Dame Stadium look like "Romper Room."

In a mostly forgotten sidelight to the contest, USC players went on a Friday-evening walk-through of the campus that they will never forget. McDonald recalled that the Trojans had to have a police escort as hundreds of LSU fans, many of them drinking, jeered the team. Former NFL great Lott indicated that the Trojans were lucky to get out of Baton Rouge in one piece, considering the crowd hysteria that marked the game. He also remarked that the atmosphere in Tiger Stadium was the loudest and scariest that he ever encountered in his illustrious football career, including several Super Bowl contests. He said that it was the only game where he had been intimidated by a crowd.

LSU would end the season unranked with a 7-5 record but gave the departing McClendon a 34-10 victory over Wake Forest in the Tangerine Bowl. Even with the loss, the USC game ranks second as one of the greatest games played in Tiger Stadium. On crowd noise and sheer drama alone, some rate it first.

NUMBER 3: THE POKER GAME
LSU 28, Florida 24: October 6, 2007

It was a game for the ages in Tiger Stadium as number-one LSU gambled five times on fourth down and converted every one to defeat defending national champion Florida and Heisman Trophy winner Tim Tebow, 28-24.

A couple of days before the game, some LSU fans discovered Tebow's cell-phone number and rained down mocking calls on the quarterback. Not intimidated, Tebow ran toward the LSU student section during a break in the game and placed his hand to his ear to mimic a cell-phone call. After the contest, however, the signal caller would say that the razor-thin loss to LSU that evening was one of the most excruciating of his career.

Behind 10 points in the fourth quarter, LSU gutted out one of its greatest wins in Tiger Stadium. The crowd went berserk when the announcer broke the news that number-two Southern California had lost to 41-point underdog Stanford, 24-23. LSU's defense, which had been hammered for three quarters by Tebow and the Gator running backs, stood tall in the fourth quarter, forcing two Florida turnovers that provided the margin of victory.

Jacob Hester, Shreveport, Louisiana, native and later an NFL fullback, was unstoppable when the downs counted the most. He saved his best for a 2-yard blast up the middle on fourth down for the winning touchdown with only seconds remaining. The hard-charging back finished the night with 106 yards on twenty-six carries. Hester said the Gators knew what was coming, even calling out the plays, but the Tiger offensive line was determined to move them off the ball. The running back said the Tigers ran a lot of ball control to keep Tebow and his outstanding offense off the field as much as possible.

The record crowd of 92,910 was not able to breathe a sigh of relief, though, until a desperation pass by Tebow was knocked down in the LSU end zone with no time remaining on the clock. The Tigers whipped the Gators in the battle of statistics, too, with twenty-five first downs to Florida's nineteen. LSU gained 391 total yards to the Gators' 314. A big statistic for the Tigers was holding Tebow to 67 yards on sixteen carries.

With this game, Head Coach Les Miles earned his nickname, "The Mad Hatter." Because his unorthodox play calling during the 2007 season placed the Tigers in the upper echelon of college football, he will forever be a legend in the minds of many LSU faithful.

LSU would go on that season to win the BCS National Championship in New Orleans, despite having overtime losses to Arkansas and Kentucky. Getting many of its injured players back for the national title game, the Tigers brushed aside number-one Ohio State, 38-24, in a game that wasn't as close as the score.

LSU's Jacob Hester lunges into the Florida end zone to give the Tigers the victory. (AP Photo/Bill Haber)

A dejected Tim Tebow walks off the Tiger Stadium field in 2007. (AP Photo/Bill Haber)

Hester waves to the crowd after helping LSU defeat Florida in 2007. (AP Photo/Alex Brandon)

LSU fans wildly cheer on the Bayou Bengals. (AP Photo)

NUMBER 4: THE EARTHQUAKE GAME
LSU 7, AUBURN 6: OCTOBER 8, 1988

It was the night the ground actually shook in Tiger Stadium. Yes, an earthquake was recorded on the night of October 8, 1988, when LSU quarterback Tommy Hodson threw a touchdown pass to running back Eddie Fuller with 1:41 left to play in a 7-6 victory over Auburn.

Some Tiger players said they could actually feel the vibrations under their feet when Fuller caught the ball. LSU graduate and golf great David Toms stated that it was the biggest roar he had ever heard in Tiger Stadium. In fact, it was so loud that a 2.7-magnitude earthquake was recorded on a seismograph on the LSU campus that evening.

Dennis Laughlin, an LSU fan since 1987, described the scene that night as unbelievable. "I have never been so energized in my life. People were jumping up and down. There was a lot of yelling and screaming . . . everybody was just going nuts," he said.

For most of the game, Auburn's tenacious defense had kept LSU in check. Until six minutes remained in the game, LSU's offense had gained only 138 yards and eight first downs. The Tigers had punted eleven times. But with the clock ticking away and no timeouts, Hodson hit

Tiger Stadium was the scene of the only earthquake recorded on a campus during a college football game. (AP Photo/Aaron M. Sprecher)

three different receivers and drove LSU from its 24-yard line to the Auburn 11-yard line. With the game at stake, Hodson was facing fourth and 10 when he connected with Fuller in the end zone and the crowd went crazy.

First to discover just how crazy the crowd went that night was Riley Milner, a member of the Louisiana Geological Survey team. Visiting the Howe-Russell Geosciences Complex on Monday, he noticed something unusual—a very distinct recording on the seismograph. After the instrument was taken to a seismic researcher on the campus, the experts realized that the recording was timed perfectly with the touchdown, according to an article written by an LSU student.

Thus, "The Earthquake Game" of 1988 became part of the folklore of Tiger Stadium that has continued for decades. Fuller said he didn't think much about the game until he saw it featured at a Ripley's Believe It or Not Museum in Niagara Falls in the early 1990s.

Both Hodson and Fuller later recalled it as the most physically punishing game of their college careers. The loss at Tiger Stadium probably kept an outstanding Auburn team from winning the national championship that season. LSU finished the 1988 season at 8-4, losing the Hall of Fame Bowl in Tampa, Florida, to Syracuse, 23-10.

Hodson, considered one of LSU's greatest signal callers, started four years for the Tigers. He owns a career-record 8,938 yards for a quarterback in a season at LSU and the most career touchdowns at sixty-nine. Hodson was not only an outstanding passer but also a runner who could make valuable yardage if receivers were covered.

The 1988 Bengal defense produced a galaxy of stars who moved on to the NFL. Some of them were All-American safety Greg Jackson, who played for the Philadelphia Eagles, New Orleans Saints, and San Diego Chargers; defensive end Kenny Davidson, who played for the Pittsburgh Steelers and Houston Oilers; defensive tackle Marc Boutte, who had a career with the Los Angeles Rams and Washington Redskins; defensive tackle Karl Dunbar, who played for the Arizona Cardinals and New Orleans Saints; linebacker Eric Hill, who starred many years for the Arizona Cardinals; and nose guard Darrell Phillips, a member of the All-SEC Team in 1988. The late Ralph Norwood was an All-SEC offensive tackle who played for the Atlanta Falcons.

Florida's Steve Spurrier took it on the chin at Tiger Stadium in 1997. (AP Photo/Rick Bowmer)

NUMBER 5: THE X'S AND O'S GAME
LSU 28, FLORIDA 21: OCTOBER 11, 1997

In one of the most momentous games played in Tiger Stadium, LSU defeated a number-one team in Baton Rouge for the very first time. And it was Florida. And it was Steve Spurrier.

An uncontrollable crowd broke down a chain-link fence surrounding the field as the final horn sounded. The fans then tore down the goalposts, wiping away years of frustration at the hands of Florida and Spurrier.

LSU quarterback Herb Tyler said the coaches had them very prepared to pull the upset, with new Xs and Os drawn up by Head Coach Gerry DiNardo and Defensive Coach Carl Reese.

The Tigers won the stunner with a brand-new trap play. Running right at the middle of the Florida line, Kevin Faulk gained 78 yards and fullback Tommy Banks—a crowd favorite with his tremendous bulk—gained 34 yards. Tyler, a cool customer with the ball in his hands, gained 50 yards and scored two touchdowns on keepers while passing for 172 yards with ten completions in seventeen attempts.

Reese, meanwhile, brought back the Chinese Bandits in a substitution plan that kept the Tiger defenders well rested. The defensive game package brought Gator quarterback Doug Johnson down five times and intercepted him four times. All-American guard Alan Faneca drove Gators off the ball time and time again, making big holes for the Tiger backs to charge through.

With the score knotted at 14-14 and fourteen minutes remaining in the third quarter, Johnson threw a pass that was intercepted by LSU defensive back Cedric Donaldson. Donaldson ran it back untouched into the Gator end zone, giving the Tigers a 21-14 lead. He also had another interception, broke up four passes, and made ten tackles.

Not to be outdone in the momentous upset, backfield teammate Chris Cummings

All-American Alan Faneca was a beast against Florida in 1997. (AP Photo/Rich Schultz)

blocked a field goal, tipped four passes, and made thirteen tackles. With these efforts, the Tiger defense disrupted the Gator offense all night.

Voted as the top night game in Tiger Stadium history in an LSUsports.net fan poll, LSU ended Florida's twenty-five-game winning streak in the Southeastern Conference in shocking fashion.

Other players of note from 1997 were All-American punter Chad Kessler; All-American offensive lineman Nacho Albergamo; All-American defensive tackle Anthony "Booger" McFarland, who anchored the line; and Cecil "the Diesel" Collins, an outstanding running back who later ran afoul of the law and left football.

The Tigers would finish the season with a 9-3 mark, losing to Notre Dame, Ole Miss, and Auburn. However, they defeated the Irish 27-9 in a rematch at the Independence Bowl in Shreveport, Louisiana.

NUMBER 6: THE REVENGE GAME THAT WASN'T

ALABAMA 21, LSU 17: NOVEMBER 3, 2012

LSU had everything it wanted. The game was at night, when the Tigers rarely lose. It was the biggest crowd to ever watch a game in Tiger Stadium. The fans were delirious. Revenge for the Tigers' embarrassing 21-0 championship loss to Alabama the previous season was going to be sweet. Motivation was off the charts. Every college-football fan in the nation was watching. The Bayou Bengals were ready to play.

And the Tigers did win the first 59:09 minutes of the game, with a big margin in yards gained and time of possession.

But Alabama won the game.

The agony of defeat had never been so great for LSU fans, players, and coaches in the stadium where "teams come to die." On this night, a young secondary for the Tigers was swallowed up in the last 1:34 of the game by determined Alabama quarterback AJ McCarron and his receivers. He threw six completions in 51 seconds for sixty-three yards, driving a knife through the hearts of Tiger players and fans.

LSU quarterback Zach Mettenberger played the game of his life. With the ball deep in Tide territory and time running out, he drove the Tigers to pound in what looked like the last nail in Alabama's coffin. But a strange thing happened. Mettenberger, who had taken the Tigers down the field with precision passing, gave way to a running game against the Tide's stacked defense in an attempt to run out the clock. Since LSU could not run the ball successfully against a bunched line such as Alabama's, the Tigers made little or no gain on three running plays. Then Drew Alleman missed a fifty-four-yard field goal. Had the Tigers elected to punt, Alabama might have started inside its ten-yard line.

AJ McCarron put a knife through the hearts of the Tigers in 2012. (AP Photo/Dave Martin)

LSU's Zach Mettenberger had his best game in 2012 against Alabama. (AP Photo/Bill Haber)

Certainly, questionable and very conservative play calling contributed to the Tigers' downfall at the end of the game, despite their hard fight for revenge against the Tide. Instead of moving the ball on Mettenberger's strong right arm, the Tigers went to a costly running game when a spread offensive may have kept them on the field long enough to run out the clock. Part of the blame for the loss would fall on the LSU offensive minds. The Tide knew exactly what the Tigers were going to do, and that was run the ball up the middle. It didn't work. Of course, LSU's young secondary would take partial blame for the collapse at the end of the contest as defense assignments were missed, Miles said.

McCarron was not brilliant on this Saturday night in Death Valley, but he only needed to be when it counted the most and he fulfilled that obligation. Kept in check for most of the evening, the Alabama quarterback assaulted the LSU two-minute defense with a sixty-three-yard winning drive that stunned the overflow crowd into silence. McCarron said he had scouted what the Tigers deployed in similar situations and had put together the drive by watching film.

Trailing 14-3 at halftime, the Tigers looked as though they would be roughed up by the Tide again, as they had been on January 7. But LSU came out after the break looking like a completely different team, physically beating Alabama at the line of scrimmage. Mettenberger was on fire, hitting fourteen of seventeen passes for 201 yards in the second half and completing twenty-four of thirty-six passes for the game and a career-high 298 yards. But the old slogan of "dance with the one who brought you" went out the window in the last minute, allowing the Tide to come back and win the game.

Mettenberger wasn't the only LSU player having an outstanding game against the Tide. Jarvis Landry had eight catches for 76 yards, and freshman sensation Jeremy Hill rushed for 107 yards and a third-quarter touchdown that got the Tigers back in the game. Despite these plays, the Tigers lost to the Tide in a game they should have won and had circled on their calendar.

The Tigers had held a 9-4 winning edge over the Tide in regular-season games since 2000. Alabama's domination over LSU had finally come to an end beginning with the new century. However, two straight losses to the Tide distorted those figures and made Alabama the reigning national champion for two straight years and three out of four years.

Although expectations were not met in 2012, the future looked very bright for LSU, with the coaching hire of offensive coordinator Cam Cameron in 2013, a former NFL coordinator. Also, the continued presence of defensive wizard John Chavis, who molded a bevy of LSU and Tennessee players into pro defense stars, would certainly remain a factor. Add in the recruiting of Les Miles and his great winning percentage at LSU, and the Tigers had the ingredients for a national top team every year.

Coach Dietzel knew that the Gators would be a huge challenge in 1958. (AP Photo)

NUMBER 7: THE "WE ARE NUMBER ONE" GAME
LSU 10, Florida 7: October 25, 1958

A tremendous struggle in Tiger Stadium between two SEC heavyweights in 1958 vaulted the Tigers to number one in the nation for the very first time in the modern era. And LSU remained on top until being upset by Tennessee in Knoxville in a 1959 game that could have been won if not for a rash of turnovers by the Tigers.

On the road to their first national championship and only undefeated season in modern times, the Tigers encountered three big roadblocks. The first was the Florida Gators, one of the few SEC teams that could almost match the Tigers' depth and talent. The second was Mississippi, ranked number six, whom the Tigers played the next week at home and defeated 14-0, following a dramatic goal-line stand. Despite the score, most viewers said the game could have gone either way. The third and most serious challenge was the Mississippi State Bulldogs. LSU barely escaped 7-6 after taking a mud bath in treacherous conditions at Starkville.

As most students of college football know, it takes a lot of skill but also some luck to win a national championship, which was certainly the case for the Bayou Bengals in 1958. The Tigers were facing a Florida team with an outstanding defense, and the superior depth they held over most teams would not apply against the Gators. Holding teams to sixty-five yards rushing per game, Florida was led by Head Coach Bob Woodruff, who had Dietzel's number up until this game.

The pregame hype was off the charts, as one of the most boisterous crowds in Tiger Stadium up to that time attended the contest. The game turned into a brutal battle of defensive giants. Florida dominated the statistics; LSU, the field position. If the Tigers were going to win the contest, it would be by the smallest of margins. With time running out, the Bayou Bengals marched to the Gators' nineteen-yard line, mostly on Cannon's power running up the middle.

With 2:59 left in the game, Dietzel elected to call on Go Team tailback and outstanding placekicker Tommy Davis

Tommy Davis helped LSU defeat Florida with a field goal in the waning minutes of the 1958 contest. (AP Photo/ NFL Photos)

for a field goal to win. Davis split the uprights, and LSU's winning streak and the march toward the national championship continued. The Tigers would go 11-0, defeating Clemson 7-0 in the Sugar Bowl when Mickey Mangham caught a nine-yard touchdown pass from running back Billy Cannon in the third quarter.

LSU had several standouts on its first national-championship team. Heisman Trophy winner Billy Cannon went on to have a great pro career with the Houston Oilers and other professional teams. Leading the AFC twice in rushing yards, he also played with the Oakland Raiders as an All-Pro tight end before finishing up with the Kansas City Chiefs in 1970. The All-American had his LSU jersey, number 20, retired. Cannon was elected to the College Football Hall of Fame in 2008. The vote came late, following a counterfeit scheme that landed him in prison. However, the Heisman winner was later accepted back into the LSU family. He appeared at many Tiger games, where he was loudly cheered for his exploits on the Tiger gridiron.

The late Mickey Mangham was an All-SEC player for the Tigers at both offensive and defensive end. He was also an Academic All-American. He concluded his college career in the 1960 Blue-Gray Football Classic, scoring the only touchdown of the game on a sixteen-yard reception.

Johnny Robinson was an outstanding running and defensive back with the Tigers and safety with the Kansas City Chiefs from 1960 to 1972. A first-round draft pick, he was a nine-time AFL All Star with the Chiefs. He was named to the AFL's All-Time Team, the Pro Football Hall of Fame Team of the 1960s decade, the Kansas City Chiefs' All-Time Team, and the Louisiana Sports Hall of Fame. He founded and still operates a youth home for troubled boys in Monroe, Louisiana.

The late Tommy Davis was a kicker and running back for the Go Team. Drafted by the San Francisco 49ers, he played ten years for the team and was selected to the pro bowl for two seasons. In the NFL, Davis made 130 field goals and had 22,833 punting yards, 82 yards being his longest.

Johnny Robinson was a star on both the offensive and defensive sides of the ball for LSU in the late 1950s. (AP Photo/NFL Photos)

The late Mel Branch played with the Chinese Bandits during his career as a defensive end at LSU. From 1960 to 1968, he played with the Kansas City Chiefs and Miami Dolphins.

Tight end Billy Hendrix was All-SEC in 1958. He is mostly remembered for his dramatic touchdown catch against Mississippi State, which allowed the Tigers to slip past the Bulldogs 7-6 and remain unbeaten.

All-American offensive center and linebacker Max Fugler is recalled for his heroics against Ole Miss in 1958, when he helped stop the Rebels from the LSU one-foot yard line on four consecutive plays. Drafted by the San Francisco 49ers, he suffered a severe knee injury in his rookie season that ended his playing career.

Warren Rabb was an All-SEC quarterback for the Tigers in the late 1950s. (AP Photo)

Charles "Bo" Strange was an outstanding offensive lineman for the Tigers, making the All-SEC team three times. He was selected to the Louisiana State Athletic Hall of Fame in 1978. Strange later became an orthopedic surgeon in Baton Rouge, Louisiana.

Warren Rabb was an All-SEC quarterback with the Tigers in 1958. Playing both ways, he is remembered for his goal-line stop, along with Cannon, of Ole Miss quarterback Doug Elmore in 1959, saving the game for the Tigers. In the pros, he played for the Detroit Lions and Buffalo Bills.

Lynn LeBlanc was an All-SEC tackle with the Tigers, also serving as team captain. The late fullback J. W. "Red" Brodnax was a terrific blocker and was named most valuable player on the team for 1958. He later played for the Pittsburgh Steelers and Denver Broncos. Other notable players on the team were Gus Kinchen, Tommy Lott, Tommy Neck, Andy Bourgeois, Donnie Daye, Dave McCarty, Don "Scooter" Purvis, Ed McCreedy, Larry Kahlden, Henry Lee Roberts, Darryl Jenkins, Hart Bourque, Merle Schexnaildre, Duane Leopard, Scott McClain, Al Dampier, Jack Frayer, Bobby Greenwood, Durel Matherne, Mike Stupka, John Langan, and Emile Fournet.

All-American Roy Winston was a standout offensive guard for LSU in 1961. (AP Photo/NFL Photos)

NUMBER 8: THE "GO TO HELL" GAME
LSU 10, Ole Miss 7: November 4, 1961

It was a game that legendary Ole Miss coach Johnny Vaught, coming into Tiger Stadium, believed LSU had no chance of winning . . . or at least that's what he said. Before the game, he stated that his team was confident and that the players didn't think anyone could beat them. After all, weren't his Rebels ranked number one in the nation? Didn't he have plenty of seniors back from the squad that had defeated LSU 21-0 in the 1960 Sugar Bowl? Wasn't his team unchallenged and well rested for this contest?

The Ole Miss coach failed to realize that his team was encountering an extremely talented Tiger contingent that, in the mind of some football experts, was the best to ever suit up for the Purple and Gold. LSU would lose its only game, the first one, on a rainy night to the Rice Owls in Houston, Texas, 16-3, after committing several costly turnovers. Rice, in those days, was a Southwest Conference powerhouse, often filling its stadium with over seventy thousand fans for various games, including the LSU contests.

LSU entered the game at 5-1, having won five straight contests with its tenacious defense, while Ole Miss stood unchallenged at 6-0. The LSU-Ole Miss rivalry was at its zenith in 1961. Students were so pumped up for the game that, when a bus carrying the Rebel team arrived on campus Friday afternoon, Tiger fans surrounded the vehicle and, by some accounts, attempted to turn it over. Hearing "Go to hell, Ole Miss; go to hell," Rebel players stayed on the bus until they thought it was safe to head into the locker room.

Vaught was right about one thing—his team had superior talent as it outgained the Tigers 322-213 yards with eleven more first downs and a big margin in time of possession. But he was wrong about the only thing that counted. The Tigers were able to pull off a 10-7 thriller before an overflow crowd of 68,000 rabid fans after LSU caused two fourth-quarter Ole Miss turnovers. "I hope the boys on the 1958 and 1959 teams will forgive me, but this is the greatest victory I've been associated with," Dietzel told the press after the game.

Leading to the win was a fifty-seven-yard blast by Jerry Stovall around the right end to the Rebel twenty-three in the second half. In the drive, LSU made its only pass completion of the night when Billy Truax made a diving catch from quarterback Lynn Amedee at the Rebel twelve-yard line. Two plays later, Wendell Harris ran into the end zone untouched on a trick play, notching the victory.

LSU would go undefeated the rest of 1961, winning the SEC championship and beating Colorado 25-7 in the Orange Bowl, Dietzel's last game at LSU before heading to Army. Dietzel, who many times had said he "would never leave LSU," would return later as the school's athletic director. Living in Baton Rouge, the former coach stayed in the limelight through public and game appearances and by writing college-football books.

Offensive stars on the Tiger team that year included All-American offensive guard Roy Winston and running backs Wendell Harris, Jerry Stovall, and Earl Gros. Stovall would finish second in the Heisman Trophy voting in 1962. A defensive stalwart was All-American Fred Miller at tackle from Homer, Louisiana.

Stovall, the second overall pick for the St. Louis Cardinals in the 1963 draft, would star for many years as a defensive back for the team, making the pro bowl in the 1966-67 and

Stovall's fifty-seven-yard blast helped LSU defeat the Rebels in a big 1961 upset. (AP Photo)

1969 seasons. The former LSU football coach was also elected to the College Football Hall of Fame.

Harris, who could play many positions, would be a first-round draft choice by the Baltimore Colts and would play later for the New York Giants. At LSU, he was also a placekicker.

Gros, a six-foot-three-inch, 220-pound sledgehammer with speed, was a first-round draft choice by the Green Bay Packers. The running back also played for the Pittsburgh Steelers, Philadelphia Eagles, and New Orleans Saints. He finished an outstanding pro career with 3,157 yards rushing and 1,255 yards receiving.

Miller, who at first didn't consider professional football, was drafted by the Baltimore Colts and selected to the pro bowl for three straight seasons in 1967-69. He played on the 1971 Super Bowl team that defeated Dallas. The defensive tackle may be more famous, though, for playing high-school football for the Homer, Louisiana, "Iron Men" in 1957.

Because of injuries, the group dressed out only seventeen players at times and thus earned the nickname. Winning games against all odds, the team would also send running back Ray Wilkins and left tackle Bobby Flurry to LSU, and twelve players would receive college scholarships.

Other outstanding players on the Tigers were left end Gene Sykes, center Dennis Gaubatz, right guard Monk Guillot, right tackle Billy Joe Booth, quarterback Jimmy Field, left end Danny Neumann, All-American right end Billy Truax, running back Bo Campbell, left tackle Bobby Flurry, left end Robby Hucklebridge, right end Mike Morgan, left halfback Tommy Neck, right halfback Buddy Soefker, and fullback Buddy Hamic.

Without question, the 1961 Purple and Gold team must be considered, along with a few other Bengal contingents, one of the greatest LSU teams.

NUMBER 9: THE "ON THE ROAD TO GLORY" GAME
LSU 17, GEORGIA 10: SEPTEMBER 20, 2003

It was the year that LSU fans had been waiting for since 1958. Although the Tigers had one of the greatest stadiums and fan bases in the country, it had had no national championship to brag about in nearly half a century.

In the 2000 season, Nick Saban from Michigan State, the coach that many Tiger fans would later come to disdain, immediately began to work his magic at LSU, with savvy coaching and great recruiting. He did something that no coach since 1969 had been able to do in Tiger Stadium—beat Alabama. In his second year, Saban won an SEC crown, and in his fourth season, the 2003 national championship. The Tigers were grabbing the national spotlight once again.

Before LSU could take that crown home, though, it had to get past a tenacious Georgia team, ranked number seven in the nation and featuring star quarterback David Green and a group of talented receivers. The eleventh-ranked Tigers were 3-0 and considered an up-and-coming team. LSU would find out just how good it was against Georgia after hammering three lightweight opponents in non-conference action.

A classic defensive struggle ensued. Georgia would take a 3-0 lead into the second quarter on a thirty-three-yard Billy Bennett field goal. LSU would finally score with three minutes left in the half on a Shyrone Carey twenty-one-yard scamper. In the third quarter, LSU's Ryan Gaudet would make a forty-seven-yard field goal, giving the Tigers a 10-3 lead. That score remained until a furious rally by both teams late in the game.

Recovering a fumble by LSU quarterback Matt Mauck on the Georgia seven-yard line, the Bulldogs went to work. Very quickly the game was tied as Green threw a screen pass to Tyson Browning, who went for ninety-three yards and a touchdown. With only a couple of minutes left, the game looked as if it might go into overtime, but the Tigers were not through scoring either. With 1:22 remaining, Mauck would throw a touchdown pass to Skyler Green instead of Michael Clayton, who was supposed to receive the pass. Quarterback Green would get the ball back one more time for Georgia but would throw an interception, ending the game.

Thus, the Tigers would gut out a great victory over Georgia, even though the Bulldogs led in practically every statistical category. The Bulldogs would net 411 total yards to the Tigers' 285. Georgia would also lead in first downs, 23-16. Although Green passed for 314 yards, he was only twenty of forty-six with two interceptions. Mauck was fourteen of twenty-nine with one interception. Shyrone Carey would lead the Tigers in rushing, with 73 yards on eighteen carries.

With this victory over an outstanding Georgia team, observers started to wonder just how far this LSU team could go. After the Tigers lost to Florida at home, 19-7, some were thinking not very far. But they discounted an LSU team that would win the rest of its games.

After the Bengals captured the SEC West title, first up was Georgia again, winner of the Eastern Division. The question was could the Tigers beat an outstanding team two times in a season, especially since the game was being played in Atlanta. The answer was a resounding yes. The matchup was a 34-14 blowout, showing how much the Tigers had improved over the course of the season.

LSU quarterback Matt Mauck celebrates a big victory over Tennessee for the SEC championship in 2001. (AP Photo/Stephen Morton)

The next stop for LSU would be the BCS National Championship game in New Orleans against Oklahoma, which had one of the highest-scoring and record-setting offensive machines in college football, including a Heisman Trophy winner in Jason White at quarterback. With no problem, the Tigers handled the Sooners, 21-14. For nearly the entire contest, the Bayou Bengals totally shut down the Oklahoma offense. Only a fumble by Matt Mauck on the Sooner one-yard line kept the game close.

Many great players for LSU made up the roster in 2003 and led the Tigers to an unforgettable season, including All-American receiver Michael Clayton; All-American receiver Skyler Green; receiver Devery Henderson; All-SEC receiver Dwayne Bowe; All-SEC punt returner and receiver Craig Davis; All-American offensive lineman Stephen Peterman; offensive lineman Nate Livings; All-SEC offensive lineman Rudy Niswanger; All-SEC offensive lineman Will Arnold; All-American offensive lineman Andrew Whitworth; All-American offensive lineman Ben Wilkerson; defensive lineman Melvin Oliver; All-American defensive lineman Kyle Williams; All-American defensive lineman Chad Lavalais; All-American defensive end Marcus Spears; All-SEC freshman Kirston Pittman; All-American linebacker Brady James; linebacker Eric Alexander; linebacker Cameron Vaughn; linebacker Brian West, who later pitched for the Chicago White Sox; All-SEC linebacker Lionel Turner; All-American defensive back LaRon Landry; All-American defensive back Corey Webster; defensive back Jessie Daniels; All-American defensive back Craig Steltz; defensive back Jack Hunt; defensive back Ronnie Prude; defensive back Ryan Gilbert; All-SEC quarterback Matt Mauck; Matt Flynn, 2007 National Championship Player of the Game; All-SEC quarterback JaMarcus Russell, number-one pick of the 2008 NFL draft; quarterback Marcus Randall; running back Shyrone Carey; running back Alley Broussard; freshman All-American running back Justin Vincent; and All-SEC running back Joseph Addai. Many players from the 2003 roster are still active in the NFL, demonstrating the greatness of that LSU team.

LSU receiver Dwayne Bowe runs for yardage against Florida in a 2003 contest. (AP Photo/Phil Sandlin, file)

Bert Jones threw a last-second touchdown pass for the victory against Ole Miss in 1972.
(AP Photo)

NUMBER 10: THE TIME-WARP GAME
LSU 17, Ole Miss 16: November 4, 1972

Did time really stand still on the night of November 4, 1972, in Tiger Stadium? If you were an Ole Miss fan it did. The scoreboard read 00:01 when LSU quarterback Bert Jones threw a pass to running back Brad Davis, who juggled the ball and dove into the end zone to win the game.

Rebel fans had a reason to be angry. Ole Miss had outplayed LSU all night but was beaten as Jones tossed the ten-yard winning pass and the clock ran out. Rebel fans claimed that regulation should have ended on the previous play, explaining that there was no way three plays could be run in ten seconds.

The clock operator, James W. Campbell, Jr., of Memphis, admitted that the last few plays of the game were not handled well. He said he started the clock at the first movement of quarterback Jones because he couldn't see the precise instant of the snap. SEC officials later investigated the situation and agreed with Campbell.

Reliving the touchdown catch, Davis said he lost the ball in the lights, reached up and felt it, and then brought it into his arms. Rebel quarterback Norris Weese said the stadium "just exploded" after the score, with thousands of fans jumping high into the night air. A sign went up on the Louisiana-Mississippi border a week after the game. "Entering Louisiana, set your clocks back four seconds," it said, referring to the time it took to run the last two plays.

The Tigers would finish the season at 9-2-1, ranked number eleven in the nation. Their losses were to Alabama in the regular season and Tennessee in the Bluebonnet Bowl; the tie was with Florida.

Some standouts who emerged in 1972 were All-American cornerback Mike Williams, who played many years for the San Diego Chargers; All-American linebacker Warren Capone, who played briefly with the Dallas Cowboys and New Orleans Saints; All-SEC defensive tackle Steve Cassidy; and kicker Rusty Jackson, who played for the Los Angeles Rams and Buffalo Bills. Consensus All-American Bert Jones would later star for the Baltimore Colts, playing for eight years and leading the team to three divisional championships. He was named All-Pro and NFL Player of the Year in 1976.

Mike Williams was an All-American cornerback for LSU. (AP Photo/NFL Photos)

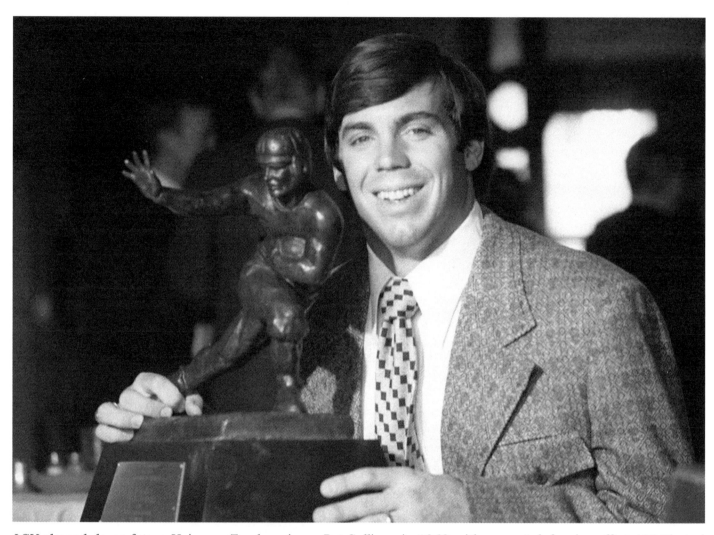

LSU slowed down future Heisman Trophy winner Pat Sullivan in 1969 with a great defensive effort. (AP Photo/ Anthony Camerano, File)

NUMBER 11: THE BLOCKED EXTRA POINT GAME
LSU 21, AUBURN 20: OCTOBER 25, 1969

In 1969, LSU fielded what many sports scribes have labeled its greatest team ever. And in October of that year, it played one its greatest games, defeating highly ranked Auburn 21-20 in a game that was a nail biter from start to finish. A daylight contest was held in order to accommodate ABC television. Any television game was a big event in 1969.

Auburn came roaring into Tiger Stadium with a record of 4-1, along with the headline-grabbing duo of future Heisman Trophy-winning quarterback Pat Sullivan and receiver Terry Beasley. LSU was 5-0 and sported four defensive All-Americans in linebackers George Bevan and Mike Anderson, defensive tackle Ronnie Estay, and defensive back Tommy Casanova. This premier unit had held three opponents to minus rushing yardage and finished the season allowing just thirty-eight rushing yards per game. The Tigers were also an offensive juggernaut, led by quarterback Mike Hillman.

The usually conservative Coach McClendon had a surprise up his sleeve for Auburn from his thirty-two on the very first play of the game. Wide receiver Andy Hamilton lined up at tight end. Hillman took the snap and pitched out to running back Jimmy Gilbert, as if the play were a toss sweep. However, Gilbert pulled up and threw a touchdown pass to Hamilton, running free in the Auburn secondary.

In what at first looked like a runaway, Auburn quickly answered and showed it had the offensive players to take on the Bengal defense. Forced to adjust to win the game, Tiger defensive coach Doug Hamley switched to a 5-2 front to get more beef on the line of scrimmage. The change of strategy helped, but Auburn went on a ninety-five-yard drive toward the end of the game and scored a touchdown, slashing the lead to one point. Suddenly, LSU's defense would have to come up with a great play to win the hard-fought contest. It did just that when linebacker Bevan blocked the extra point with his right forearm, assuring the Bengals a gut-wrenching win over the Auburn Tigers.

LSU would lose only one game that season—to Ole Miss, 26-23, in Oxford. A scrambling Archie Manning ran for big chunks of yardage after his receivers were covered. Without his ability to elude the pass rush that day, LSU might have been on the road to its second national championship. Bevan would later tell Manning at sporting events that he was still chasing him in his dreams.

The Tigers would not play in a postseason game, because the Cotton Bowl reneged on its handshake deal to line up number-one Texas against LSU. Instead, Notre Dame played the Longhorns, after the Fighting Irish decided to drop a policy of not playing in postseason games.

Other outstanding players on the 1969 roster were All-SEC safety Craig Burns, All-SEC defensive tackle John Sage, All-SEC center Godfrey Zaunbrecher, All-SEC kicker and fullback Eddie Ray, All-SEC running back Art Cantrelle, All-SEC placekicker Mark Lumpkin, and linebacker Richard Picou.

South Carolina's Steve Spurrier lets off steam in a loss to LSU in 2012. (AP Photo/Gerald Herbert)

NUMBER 12: SPURRIER HAS A DARK GAME
LSU 23, South Carolina 21: October 13, 2012

It was one of the loudest crowds at Tiger Stadium in years. The scenario was hair raising—number-three South Carolina at number-nine LSU—and the game was at night, when Bayou Bengal fans are juiced and seldom disappointed. Throw in longtime Tiger nemesis Steve Spurrier and you have a setting boiling over with anticipation.

No one came away disappointed . . . at least no LSU fan.

Although LSU dominated in the statistics, with 406 yards to Carolina's 211, the contest wasn't decided until the last seconds of the game, when the Gamecocks' quarterback Connor Shaw threw an interception near the Tiger end zone.

Tiger freshman sensation Jeremy Hill had burst through the Carolina defensive line for a fifty-yard touchdown run late in the fourth quarter to put the game on ice. The Gamecocks scored another touchdown with only 1:41 left. But it was not enough, as a rowdy crowd saw the Tigers overcome a second-half deficit in a crucial contest, upending the Gamecocks, 23-21.

A dejected Spurrier said he understood why LSU was ranked number one in preseason polls: the Tigers could both run the ball and stop the run. One of the most spectacular runners in college football, the Gamecocks' Marcus Lattimore, was held to only thirty-five yards on thirteen carries. Quarterback Shaw, both a dangerous passer and runner, was nineteen of thirty-four for two touchdowns but was intercepted twice, a statistic that probably decided the outcome of the tight contest.

Once again, LSU was stymied in the red zone, a problem the Tigers dealt with all season. Throw in the inconsistency of quarterback Zach Mettenberger, who was only twelve of twenty-five in pass completions with an interception that set up a touchdown, and it was easy to see why the game was so close. Fortunately, Hill was a workhorse for the Tigers, gaining 123 rushing yards with two touchdowns and a pass reception for 21 yards.

Meanwhile, South Carolina defensive-end terror Jadeveon Clowney had no sacks and was pretty much held in check by LSU's tattered offensive line. Shaw was sacked four times, twice by LSU defensive end Sam Montgomery, a South Carolina native.

When the final horn sounded, Tiger fans left the stadium feeling better about the team that had lost to Florida the previous week in Gainesville. However, problems would crop up for LSU again during the season, including an inconsistent offense and an offensive line that would suffer several season-ending injuries.

Three former Tiger All-Americans—from left, Tommy Casanova, Doug Moreau, and Billy Truax—sign autographs for fans in 2011 on the LSU campus. (AP Photo/Bill Haber)

NUMBER 13: THE NIGHT OF TWO MIRACLES GAME
LSU 11, OLE MISS 10: OCTOBER 31, 1964

The heyday was ending for Ole Miss in 1964, but neither team knew that, and Mississippi was ranked number one in preseason polls. The Rebels came into Tiger Stadium with losses to Kentucky and Florida, but most prognosticators thought it was just a matter of time before the squad turned it around.

It almost did against the Tigers.

LSU starting quarterback and future Baton Rouge mayor Pat Screen was injured and playing with a heavily taped knee, but he managed to take the Bayou Bengals on a sixty-nine-yard drive, hitting nine of ten passes that resulted in a field goal and a 3-0 lead. However, in the second period, the much-heralded quarterback was forced to the sidelines again, and Billy Ezell took over the signal-calling duties. Mississippi seemed to have found itself once more as LSU, punting from its goal line in the fourth quarter, trailed 10-3. As many of the disgruntled 68,000 Tiger fans headed toward the exits, the team hoped for a miracle. A miracle is just what LSU got—in fact, two of them.

As fate would have it on this night, Rebel Doug Cunningham fielded the ball on the Ole Miss forty-seven when a Tiger player knocked a Mississippi blocker into Cunningham, who fumbled the ball to LSU. With seven minutes left, the Tigers suddenly had life. Facing second down from the Mississippi nineteen-yard line, Ezell found tight end Billy Masters in the clear for a touchdown pass.

With 3:30 left in the game, LSU went for the win on a 2-point conversion attempt. McClendon later said that if more time had remained, he would have gone for the tie. But with both teams playing lights-out defense, the coach chose to go for the victory.

Providence was again on the side of LSU. Ezell would roll to the right, look toward Masters, and throw the ball to future Tiger radio analyst Doug Moreau. The ball was tipped, but Moreau made a dramatic fingertip catch and managed to stayed in bounds for a heart-pounding 11-10 Bayou Bengal victory. McClendon said he didn't realize the receiver caught the ball "until I heard the roar of the crowd."

With an 8-2-1 record, LSU would play in the Sugar Bowl and defeat Syracuse 13-10.

Many outstanding players made up the 1964 Tiger roster. Some of them were All-American offensive lineman Remi Prudhomme, who played from 1964 to 1972 with the Buffalo Bills, Kansas City Chiefs, and New Orleans Saints; the late All-American defensive tackle George Rice, with the Houston Oilers; All-American tight end Doug Moreau, with the Miami Dolphins; the late All-SEC running back Joe LaBruzzo, hero against undefeated Arkansas in the 1966 Cotton Bowl; tight end Billy Masters, with the Kansas City Chiefs, Buffalo Bills, and Denver Broncos; All-SEC linebacker Mike Vincent; All-SEC offensive linemen Dave McCormick and Richard Grainer; John Demarie, defensive tackle with the Cleveland Browns and Seattle Seahawks; and the late Billy Joe Booth, a Senior Bowl participant. Booth, who was killed in an Ontario, Canada, plane crash in 1972, was a Canadian Football League All-Star in 1969 with the Ottawa Rough Riders.

All-American Bert Jones got revenge against Notre Dame in 1971. (AP Photo)

NUMBER 14: THE REVENGE GAME
LSU 28, Notre Dame 8: November 20, 1971

Revenge was on LSU's mind for this game, as the Tigers had lost a hard-fought 3-0 game to the Irish and quarterback Joe Theismann the year before.

Much to the chagrin of many LSU fans, All-American Bert Jones had been forced to share quarterback duties with Paul Lyons for much of 1971 because of Jones' bickering with Coach McClendon. Although Lyons was a gutsy competitor and outstanding runner, he was an undersized option quarterback who lacked Jones' arm strength. But McClendon fancied signal callers who could run the option. Jones explained that McClendon would often call two running plays on first and second downs and a pass play only out of necessity. The play calling irked Jones, and he let it be known.

However, before the kickoff of this nationally televised contest, McClendon named Jones as the starter, believing that the taller quarterback could see better over the helmets of the tall Irish defensive linemen. The decision paid off. The contest was only a few minutes old when Jones connected with his first cousin Andy Hamilton for a thirty-six-yard completion and a 7-0 lead. LSU took a 14-0 lead into halftime against a team that was a 14-point favorite. Hamilton and Jones, both from the piney-woods, North Louisiana town of Ruston, proceeded to have a field day, with a pitch-and-catch performance that resulted in a 28-8 victory for LSU. In the final seconds, uncontrollable fans rushed the Tiger Stadium floor, tearing down the metal goalposts and wiping away the bitter memory of the tough loss to the Fighting Irish the previous year.

Standing tall in this game was the Tiger defense, which stopped the Irish three times inside the LSU ten-yard line, once from only a foot out.

The Irish led in every category except the scoreboard, getting eighteen first downs to LSU's fourteen and 323 yards to the Tigers' 299.

All-American defensive tackle Ronnie Estay played the game of his life against Notre Dame in 1971. (AP Photo)

"Gentlemen, there has never been a bigger victory in Tiger Stadium," McClendon told the press after the game. He would describe Jones as being both strong armed and strongwilled. Jones would later say that the highlight of his LSU career was "getting out." However, the two reportedly later reconciled.

Other stars making headlines on the 1971 team were All-American defensive back Tommy Casanova, All-American defensive tackle Ronnie Estay, All-American offensive and defensive tackle Tyler Lafauci, defensive tackles John Sage and John Wood, and receiver Gerald Keigley. Estay had one of his greatest games as a Tiger against the Fighting Irish with seventeen tackles, including thirteen solo stops. He would go down as one of the best Tiger defenders of all time due to his tremendous endurance and knack for getting to ball carriers.

LSU would finish the season 9-3, including a 33-15 victory over Iowa State in the Sun Bowl in El Paso, Texas.

NUMBER 15: THE "IT'S ABOUT TIME" GAME
LSU 30, ALABAMA 28: NOVEMBER 4, 2000

It almost seemed like a bad dream that would never go away, coming every other year. The Tigers had lost an unimaginable thirty-one home games in a row to Alabama, even though the Bayou Bengals had notched some victories on the road against the Tide. The feared Tiger Stadium brought no fear to Alabama. To put it in context, LSU had not beaten the Tide in Tiger Stadium since the United States put the first man on the moon in 1969.

But things were about to change in a big way, not just for the 2000 season but for many years to come. Starting with the new century, the Tide's domination over the Tigers would come to an abrupt end.

The much-heralded LSU quarterback Josh Booty out of Shreveport, Louisiana, didn't always live up to his potential, but on this night he did. The All-SEC Coaches quarterback came alive, throwing for 275 yards and four touchdown passes, leading the Bayou Bengals to a gut-wrenching 30-28 victory over Alabama. Thus ended the drought that had been nearly impossible for LSU fans to endure.

Josh Reed, one of LSU's all-time great receivers and future NFL star, mopped up against the Tide secondary with two touchdowns and 129 receiving yards.

Going into the fourth quarter, Tiger fans started to believe the drought might never end after the Tide took a 21-14 lead on Dustin McClintock's one-yard blast into LSU's end zone. However, with the outstanding play of Booty and running back LaBrandon Toefield, LSU took over the game during the last ten minutes, scoring 16 points to Alabama's 7.

The Tide would outgain the Tigers 164-133 yards on the ground but lose the battle in the air in a big way, 275 to 150 yards. Toefield would run for 85 yards on twenty-one carries, while Alabama's Ahmaad Galloway gained 129 yards on twenty-one rushes.

When the game was over, the crowd rushed the field and tore down a goalpost. Booty threw his arms high into the air, signaling that the long nightmare was over. A new era of LSU football had begun.

Although the Tide won only three games in 2000 after being ranked number three in preseason polls, the significance of LSU's victory cannot be overstated. Beginning with the new century, the Tigers held a 9-4 winning edge over Alabama through 2012 in regular-season games.

LSU would go on to have an up-and-down season, finishing at 8-4 but winning the Peach Bowl over Georgia Tech, 28-14. Alabama would end a dismal season losing to Central Florida at home.

Other players making headlines on the 2000 team were running back Domanick Davis, who later starred with the Houston Texans; tight end Robert Royal, who played with the Washington Redskins, Buffalo Bills, and Cleveland Browns; wide receiver and speedster Devery Henderson, a star with the New Orleans Saints; All-American linebacker Bradie James, longtime player with the Dallas Cowboys and later Houston Texans; Trev Faulk, All-SEC linebacker; Jarvis Green, longtime defensive end and Super Bowl winner with the New England Patriots; and defensive tackle Howard Green, member of several NFL teams.

LSU quarterback Josh Booty salutes LSU fans after a huge victory in 2000. (AP Photo/Bill Haber)

NUMBER 16: THE LAST-SECOND GAME
LSU 30, Auburn 24: October 20, 2007

It was another heroic finish for LSU at Tiger Stadium in 2007 as the Bayou Bengals won the game with only one second showing on the clock. Superb quarterback Matt Flynn hooked up with wide receiver Demetrius Byrd in the end zone for a stunning victory over Auburn on a night that left more than ninety-two thousand fans breathless.

Flynn finished with 319 passing yards and three touchdowns—the last one very risky, considering LSU was in field-goal range to win the game. Miles said the touchdown play was called in the last second because of the confidence he had in his players, who had roared back from a 17-7 halftime deficit.

Auburn's Brandon Cox passed for 199 yards and a pair of touchdowns, despite taking big hits from the LSU defense. His last scoring pass, a three-yard strike to Rodriques Smith, gave Auburn a 24-23 lead with 3:21 left to go in the game. But it was not enough.

LSU was forced to come from behind against an Auburn team that had ripped some gaping holes in the proud Tiger run-defense in the first half. However, the Tigers held when needed in the final stanza and found a way to win again in an amazing season of comebacks in Tiger Stadium.

Coach Miles was not afraid to gamble during the 2007 national-championship run. (AP Photo)

LSU quarterback Matt Flynn runs for a touchdown in 2007. (AP Photo/Alex Brandon)

Pat Stuckey, an LSU alum who attended the game, said he felt the "whole stadium trembling" when the Tigers scored the winning touchdown with one second remaining. "The Jack Daniel's went down a lot easier after they scored that last touchdown," the construction-engineering grad recalled.

LSU dominated in the statistics, with twenty-three first downs to Auburn's sixteen. The Tigers gained 488 yards to Auburn's 293. LSU's average gain per play was 7.2 yards to only 4.7 for Auburn. Back from an injury that had forced him out of six straight games, All-SEC receiver Early Doucet had seven catches for 93 yards, while Byrd had 89 yards on just three catches.

The victory put LSU in command of the SEC West Division over Auburn and Alabama. The Tigers would go on to win their second national championship in four years.

Quarterback Flynn would move on to set franchise records for the Green Bay Packers in a game on January 1, 2012, with 480 yards passing and six touchdowns in a victory over the Detroit Lions.

An array of stars represented the 2007 BCS National Champions, including two All-Americans: defensive tackle Glen Dorsey, drafted by the Kansas City Chiefs, and offensive lineman Herman Johnson. Other outstanding players on the team were All-SEC nose tackle Drake Nevis, drafted by the Indianapolis Colts; All-SEC linebacker Kelvin Sheppard, taken by the Buffalo Bills; All-SEC punter Patrick Fisher; All-SEC offensive lineman Ciron Black; All-SEC receiver Early Doucet, drafted by the Arizona Cardinals; and All-SEC receiver Brandon LaFell, taken by the Carolina Panthers.

LSU's stout defense held All-American Nebraska quarterback Vince Ferragamo and the number-one Cornhuskers to only six points in 1976. (AP Photo)

NUMBER 17: THE STALEMATE GAME
LSU 6, NEBRASKA 6: SEPTEMBER 11, 1976

A tie is like kissing your sister, McClendon railed, but most LSU fans felt okay about this stalemate, because Nebraska was ranked number one in the nation and was a 13-point favorite.

With 70,446 hopeful fans jammed into Tiger Stadium, the Cornhuskers got on the board early in the game with All-American and future NFL quarterback Vince Ferragamo throwing a thirteen-yard pass for a touchdown. The PAT failed on a bobbled snap, and LSU's tenacious defense shut down Nebraska and the much-heralded Ferragamo for the rest of the contest. The Tigers tacked on field goals in the third and fourth quarters to gain the tie. A raucous crowd thought LSU had won this one, but Mike Conway missed a forty-four-yard field goal wide left by inches in the final seconds.

The game is considered one of the better contests played in Tiger Stadium because of the unrelenting trench warfare waged by the lines of both schools, leaving fans somewhat dazed at the end of the game. Tiger fans left the game sapped of energy from the muggy night and close contest but, nevertheless, somewhat content to have tied with the mighty and number-one-ranked Cornhuskers. LSU went on to have an outstanding defensive unit that season but lacked a passing game, leading to a 6-4-1 record. Nebraska outgained LSU 169 to 131 in total yards that night, although the Tigers outrushed the Huskers.

A star running back for LSU in 1976 was Terry Robiskie, named SEC Most Valuable Player for the season. He was the first Tiger running back to gain over 200 yards in a single game, running for 214 yards in thirty attempts against Rice in 1976 and over a 1,000 yards for the year.

Four others players of note from the 1976 team were offensive tackle Robert Dugas, a two-time All-American selection and Louisiana Hall of Famer who would later open holes for another All-American player, running back Charles Alexander; All-SEC center John Ed Bradley, author and all-time rabid LSU Tiger fan; and standout defensive tackles A. J. Duhe and Dan Alexander.

LSU fans mob quarterback Rohan Davey after a huge SEC victory. (AP Photo/Bill Haber)

NUMBER 18: THE REDEMPTION GAME
LSU 38, TENNESSEE 31: SEPTEMBER 30, 2000

In one of the most memorable victories in Tiger Stadium, LSU defeated highly ranked Tennessee after losing the previous week to heavy underdog Alabama-Birmingham. The Tigers were the laughingstock of the national media and had something to prove. And so did quarterback Rohan Davey, who had his coming-out party in this game, passing for four touchdowns and 318 yards. LSU fans would tear down the goalposts in the thriller that went into overtime before a packed house.

Davey proved to be one of greatest signal callers of all time for the Purple and Gold. He was the only LSU quarterback to throw for more than three thousand yards in a season and to have more than three hundred yards in three consecutive games. He got the nod against the Vols because starter Josh Booty was injured. A heavily recruited player out of Miami, Davey said LSU fans energized him with their fervor for the team. Certainly the behemoth quarterback, at six-foot-five and 260 pounds, energized LSU fans.

Getting off to a quick start, the Tigers made it look like an early runaway. They took a 24-6 lead on a seventy-four-yard gallop by LaBrandon Toefield, two receiving touchdowns by Josh Reed, and a John Corbello field goal. Tennessee, attempting to show it deserved its high ranking, roared back to outscore the Bayou Bengals 25-7 in the second half, forcing overtime.

After winning the coin toss, the Volunteers elected to play defense. On the first snap, Davey found tight end Robert Royal open for a twenty-five-yard touchdown. Driving to the LSU four-yard line on the next series, Tennessee faced a fourth down with the game on the line. Hurried by three Tiger defenders, quarterback A. J. Suggs threw an incomplete pass, and suddenly many of the 91,682 Tiger fans were storming the field, uprooting the goalposts and carrying them out of the stadium.

The Tigers would wrap up an 8-4 campaign in the 2000 season with a 28-14 victory over Georgia Tech in the Peach Bowl in Atlanta, Georgia. A highly successful decade that included two national championships was just beginning for LSU.

Petrino gets upset at Miles for kicking a late field goal against Arkansas in 2011. (AP Photo/Aaron M. Sprecher)

NUMBER 19: THE HOGTIED GAME
LSU 41, ARKANSAS 17: NOVEMBER 25, 2011

In 2011, number-one-ranked LSU played one of its most significant games in Tiger Stadium, against number-three Arkansas. The undefeated Tigers had everything hinging on the outcome—a possible BCS bowl bid, which they later accepted after blasting Georgia, 42-10, and the SEC West crown. The high-flying Hogs came into Baton Rouge on a ten-game winning streak, with the Razorback faithful contending they had the best quarterback and receivers in the league. That might have been the case, but the Hogs knew who had the best team after the final tally read LSU 41, Arkansas 17.

After getting off to a shaky start and trailing 14-0, the Tigers hit the accelerator and ran over the Arkansas Razorbacks, sacking the quarterback numerous times and holding down the talented pass receivers. Senior quarterback Jordan Jefferson had one of his best outings as a Tiger signal caller, completing eighteen of twenty-nine passes for 207 yards and one touchdown.

Heisman Trophy finalist Tyrann "the Honey Badger" Mathieu got the Tigers back in the hunt on a crafty ninety-two-yard punt return. LSU tailback Kenny Hilliard said the Tigers came out in the second half with a different attitude and pounded the ball right at the middle of the Razorbacks. Hilliard, who ran the ball up the gut of Arkansas for 102 yards on nineteen carries, stated that he "really felt it out there" on that Friday in Tiger Stadium. Following LSU All-American Morris Claiborne's interception of a pass by Hog quarterback Tyler Wilson, Jefferson ran a draw play up the middle for a forty-eight-yard touchdown, putting the game out of reach at 38-17.

LSU would win a record twelve games for a season with the victory over Arkansas, extending that number to thirteen with a shellacking of Georgia in the SEC championship game. Some football commentators had billed the Arkansas game as the biggest in Tiger Stadium since LSU defeated Ole Miss 7-3 in 1959, which was also a contest between the number one and three teams in the nation. Of course, this contest lacked the excitement of that game after the Bayou Bengals went for the Hogs' jugular in the second half.

A sidelight to the game was CBS cameras catching Arkansas head coach Bobby Petrino as he exploded across the field and hurled curses at Miles when LSU tacked on a field goal with five minutes left in the game, long after the contest had been decided. Miles certainly understood—and Petrino, too—that standings in the BCS were often determined by margins of victory.

In April 2012, Petrino was involved in a motorcycle crash with a twenty-five-year-old female assistant Razorback coach on board. He was fired from Arkansas for allegedly covering up an affair.

Mathieu's ninety-two-yard punt return got LSU back on track against Arkansas in 2011. (AP Photo/Bill Haber)

LSU receiver Josh Reed drives for extra yardage against Arkansas. (AP Photo/Bill Haber)

NUMBER 20: THE SLUGFEST GAME
LSU 41, ARKANSAS 38: NOVEMBER 23, 2001

In a year when LSU heavily relied on its offense to win the SEC championship, the Tigers overcame Arkansas in an offensive slugfest that saw the Bayou Bengals run up 41 points but almost lose because of turnovers.

Running back LaBrandon Toefield, quarterback Rohan Davey, and All-American receiver Josh Reed would lead the assault against the Hogs. Toefield galloped for 173 yards and three touchdowns, while Reed amassed 183 yards receiving. The pass-happy Davey threw for 359 yards and three touchdowns, going nineteen for thirty-three for the afternoon.

But the Tigers nearly gave the game away with Davey's four interceptions, a lost fumble, and several costly penalties. For most of the game, LSU was only stopped by its own turnovers, not by Arkansas, who had come into the contest riding a six-game winning streak.

On the first possession, Toefield broke through the middle of the Arkansas line for sixty-two yards and a 7-0 lead. Scoring went back and forth in the first half, with the Tigers holding a 20-19 edge at halftime.

LSU amassed a 41-25 lead with 8:21 left in the game. However, the Razorbacks answered the wake-up call with the outstanding play of quarterback Zak Clark. Driving eighty yards in six plays, he found a receiver in the end zone and cut the deficit to 41-31. A 2-point conversion attempt failed. Holding the Tigers to a three and out on the next series, the Hogs got back on the scoreboard with a fifteen-yard touchdown pass, slashing the lead to 41-38 with 2:27 remaining in the game. However, a determined Davey was able to complete a thirty-one-yard pass to Reed on third and thirteen with less than a minute left, sealing a hard-fought victory for LSU.

The Tigers would go on to win the 2001 SEC championship with a dramatic win over heavily favored Tennessee, 31-20. LSU had lost a regular-season game to the Volunteers 26-18 in Knoxville. Davey was injured in the championship contest after being hit two yards out of bounds by a Volunteer defender, who was not flagged for the offense. However, the hit cost Tennessee dearly, because the more mobile Matt Mauck entered the game and led LSU to victory with his outstanding running skills.

The Tigers would finish the season with a 10-3 record, including a top-ten ranking and a 47-34 win over Illinois in the Sugar Bowl.

Meanwhile, Davey's biggest game in 2001 came on the road against Alabama, when he passed for 528 yards in a 35-21 victory, setting a Tiger record for passing yards in a single game. The All-SEC player would be drafted by the New England Patriots and play in a backup role for several years. In 2004, Davey would be named NFL Europe Player of the Year, winning the World Bowl with the Berlin Thunder.

Nebraska running back Mike Rozier gets three yards against LSU in the 1983 Orange Bowl. (AP Photo/Kathy Wilens)

NUMBER 21: "THE NIGHT IT RAINED ORANGES" GAME

LSU 55, FLORIDA STATE 21: NOVEMBER 20, 1982

The Tigers won the contest handily. Nevertheless, "the night it rained oranges" represented a huge victory for the LSU program against perennial power Florida State.

Head Coach Jerry Stovall and the administration deserve credit for this win, as LSU refused to play the game on national television during the day, ignoring the audience and revenue it would bring to the school. Instead, Stovall said, "Let's play them under the lights." The gutsy call to play at night paid big dividends, as LSU ground the highly regarded Seminoles into the Tiger turf.

What made the contest so important was that the winner would go to the Orange Bowl to face the very talented Nebraska Cornhuskers.

LSU dumped the veer offense that season, with Mack Brown (yes, that Mack Brown) running the offense. It produced great results. Stovall had recruited Dalton Hilliard out of Patterson, Louisiana, the year before and it brought immediate dividends, as the shifty and hard-charging tailback became one of LSU's greatest running backs.

Hilliard teamed with Garry James to form what would become known as the "Dalton-James Gang." James had blazing speed and Hilliard could turn on a dime or run over a player, presenting defenses with a nightmare. Not overly fast by today's standards, Hilliard ran a 4.6 forty but nevertheless was seldom caught from behind after hitting open space. The uncle of the bulldozing tailback Kenny Hilliard, the talented runner would go on to have an outstanding pro career with his home-state New Orleans Saints. Also having a great season was quarterback Alan Risher, who held twenty-three offensive records when his career ended at LSU. Risher would become the starting quarterback the next year for the Arizona Wranglers of the USFL.

Dalton Hilliard, one of LSU's greatest running backs, went on to star in the NFL for his home-state New Orleans Saints. (AP Photo/NFL Photos)

A surreal and eerie atmosphere engulfed Tiger Stadium as fog rolled into Baton Rouge after the contest began, reminding some fans of the LSU-Ole Miss contest of 1959. No one attending the game will ever forget the performance of freshman sensation Hilliard, who stormed the Seminole defense for 233 yards. Tiger fans began to rain down oranges onto the field after it was assured LSU had the contest in hand. Reportedly, every orange in Baton Rouge grocery stores had been sold prior to the game. If that is true, a lot of fresh screwdrivers were certainly consumed long after the contest ended.

LSU would roll up a staggering 620 yards in a game that left Florida State and Head Coach Bobby Bowden in a state of disbelief. Ecstatic fans stormed the field after the contest was over.

However, the jubilation would last only a short time for Tiger fans, as the Bayou Bengals stumbled the very next week to heavy underdog and bitter rival Tulane in Tiger Stadium, 31-28. The contest was no doubt a letdown for the Bengals after defeating Florida State the previous week, and most LSU fans were shocked by the loss.

The season would produce one other stunning victory, when the Tiger defense totally stifled the Crimson Tide in Alabama 20-10, in a contest that was not as close as the score. Alabama coach Bear Bryant said it was the worst beating his team had suffered since the 1960s. The Tigers would lose a hard-fought game to Nebraska in the Orange Bowl, 21-20.

A bevy of other stars were on the LSU football roster in 1982. They were All-American linebacker Al Richardson, with a record twenty-one tackles against South Carolina; All-American defensive tackle Leonard Marshall, who became an All-Pro selection with the New York Giants; All-SEC defensive back Eugene Daniel, who had a long career with the Indianapolis Colts; defensive back Liffort Hobley, who starred for six years with the Miami Dolphins; All-SEC defensive back James Britt, who had a five-year career with the Atlanta Falcons; running back Gene Lang, a player with the Denver Broncos and Atlanta Falcons; All-American offensive tackle Lance Smith, a longtime player with the Phoenix Cardinals; linebacker Rydell Malancon, a player with the Atlanta Falcons and Green Bay Packers; All-American receiver Eric Martin, who starred with the New Orleans Saints and Kansas City Chiefs and earned pro-bowl honors in 1988; receiver Herman Fontenot, a player with the Cleveland Browns and Green Bay Packers; All-SEC tight end Malcolm Scott; and tenacious nose guards Ramsey Dardar and Greg Bowser. With that kind of talent, it's hard to believe LSU lost any games in 1982, but talent alone doesn't win championships.

Many fans felt that the Tigers were back on track after the 8-3-1 campaign in 1982, but that was not the case. The Tigers would not win a single conference game in 1983, and Stovall would be the first in a succession of LSU coaches to be fired. The only exception was Bill Arnsparger, a legendary NFL defensive coach who would lead the Tigers to winning records from 1984 to 1986.

NUMBER 22: THE NIGHT THE IRISH FELL SHORT
LSU 21, NOTRE DAME 19: NOVEMBER 22, 1986

Two of the greatest Tigers ever to suit up for the Purple and Gold, record-setting quarterback Tommy Hodson and All-American receiver Wendell Davis, paired to take LSU to a dramatic 21-19 victory over Notre Dame and first-year head coach Lou Holtz in 1986. Seemingly out of the contest, the Fighting Irish staged a late-game comeback but failed to make a 2-point conversion with 3:32 left. The Tigers notched a slim victory before a packed and loud house of over seventy-eight thousand fans.

Redshirt freshman Hodson would have an outstanding evening for the Tigers, with three touchdown passes on 20 of 28 passing yards. Davis would have seven receptions for 128 yards and establish a single-season record mark of 1,161 yards in receptions for LSU. He would be named ESPN Player of the Game.

The number-seven Tigers got on the board first with a thirteen-yard pass from Hodson to Davis in the first quarter, but the Fighting Irish would match that on the ensuing kickoff with a ninety-six-yard return by Heisman Trophy winner Tim Brown. LSU came right back on the arm of Hodson in an eighty-two-yard, seventeen-play drive that gave the Bengals a 14-7 lead at halftime. In the third period, quarterback Steve Beuerlein began moving the Irish downfield to the LSU four-yard line, where Notre Dame cut the lead to 14-10 with a field goal.

On the next series of plays, Hodson was intercepted at the LSU thirty and had it returned to the Bengal two-yard line. But the tenacious Tiger defense—LSU's calling card for most of its existence—took over. Four cracks at the end zone lost yardage for Notre Dame, and the Purple and Goal got the ball at its own five-yard line.

Defensive tackle Henry Thomas was a huge menace for the Irish, with eleven tackles and two sacks. It was the second straight tough loss for the Irish, having fallen to number-two Penn State, 24-19, the week before. The defeat was "absolutely unbelievable," Holtz said. "What more can you tell kids after a game like this? LSU may have one of the best defenses in the nation and certainly the best coach. They attacked from all angles tonight." The Irish would defeat number-seventeen Southern Cal the following week, finishing the season 5-6.

LSU would end the year 9-3, winning the Southeastern Conference championship in Bill Arnsparger's last year at the helm of the Tigers. One of the Bayou Bengals' losses was to heavy underdog Miami of Ohio at home, 21-12, in a national shocker. However, the Tigers would defeat Florida 28-17 in Gainesville in a huge SEC game, along with beating Alabama in Birmingham, 14-10. But in an up-and-down season, the Tigers would lose at home to Ole Miss 21-19, as David Browndyke missed a chip-shot field goal at the end of the game to preserve the Rebel upset. In the Sugar Bowl, number-five LSU would fall to number-six Nebraska 30-15 in a contest that saw the Tigers set a record for the number of penalties in the annual New Orleans classic.

Defensive coordinator Mike Archer would take over the Tigers following Arnsparger's departure and lead LSU to a sparkling 10-1-1 record in 1987, with a lone loss to Alabama. Had Hodson not been injured for the Tide contest, LSU might have collected its second national championship.

Many other outstanding players were on the LSU roster in 1986. They were All-American

Notre Dame's Lou Holtz suffered a tough loss to LSU in 1986. (AP Photo/Junji Kurokawa)

offensive lineman Nacho Albergamo; two-time All-SEC nose guard Darrell Phillips; All-SEC offensive tackle Ralph Norwood; two-time All-SEC wide receiver and running back Tony Moss; All-SEC defensive back Norman Jefferson; All-SEC tight end Brian Kinchen; All-American defensive back Greg Jackson; All-SEC linebacker Eric Hill; All-SEC running back Eddie Fuller; defensive end Karl Dunbar; All-SEC linebacker Toby Caston; All-SEC defensive back Chris Carrier; All-American linebacker Michael Brooks; defensive tackle Karl Wilson; two-time All-SEC defensive tackle Roland Barbay; two-time All-SEC offensive guard Eric Andolsek; running back Harvey Williams; defensive tackle Tommy Clapp; and linebackers Oliver Lawrence and Ron Sancho.

LSU running back Kevin Faulk set a school record for rushing yards in a game against Houston in 1996.
(AP Photo/Michael Dwyer)

NUMBER 23: THE COMEBACK GAME

LSU 35, HOUSTON 34: SEPTEMBER 7, 1996

In one of the greatest comebacks in Tiger Stadium, LSU defeated the Houston Cougars, 35-34. No one thought the Bayou Bengals could win the 1996 contest after trailing 34-14 at halftime. However, they forgot to tell that to Tiger running-back great Kevin Faulk, who took over the game in the second half. Rushing for a school-record 246 yards on twenty-one carries, he returned four punts for another 106 yards around and through a weary Cougar defense.

Many LSU fans had already departed Tiger Stadium by the fourth quarter and were shocked to hear over their car radios that LSU had won the game. Those who stayed changed their chorus of boos to a rousing chorus of cheers.

The number-seventeen Tigers came into the game as 23-point favorites. They fell behind by 21 points in the early going because of five turnovers, although they led the statistical war—400 yards to 228. The final quarter saw LSU blitz the Cougars 21-0, gaining 201 yards to only 49 for Houston. The Tiger quarterback dropped to a knee at the Cougar 1-yard line with seconds left, as DiNardo elected not to run up the score.

The game did turn out to be a positive for Houston. Realizing it had played a close game against a strong LSU team, the Cougars used the contest as a stepping stone to win its first Conference USA championship.

Faulk, who had been suspended for alleged involvement in an off-season altercation outside a bar in his hometown of Carencro, Louisiana, was reinstated when the charges were dropped just before the game. Fortune was on LSU's side that day, as the Tigers would not have won the season opener without him. The Bayou Bengals would end the season 10-2, with a top-ten ranking and a victory in the Peach Bowl. All-American Faulk would finish his career at LSU with 6,833 all-purpose yards, placing him fifth on the all-time NCAA list.

David LaFleur was an All-American tight end for the Tigers in 1996. Other LSU players making headlines were offensive tackle Ben Bordelon, defense tackle Chuck Wiley, and punter Chad Kessler.

Alabama's Nick Saban gets a harsh welcome from LSU fans in the Superdome. (AP Photo/Andrew J. Cohoon, File)

NUMBER 24: THE "RETURN OF NICK SABAN" GAME
ALABAMA 27, LSU 21: NOVEMBER 8, 2008

There was no quit in these 2008 Tigers on a Saturday afternoon in Death Valley. Even with three interceptions thrown in regulation by LSU quarterback Jarrett Lee, including one that was run back for a touchdown, the Tigers battled the number-one-ranked Crimson Tide down to the wire with a chance for victory in overtime. LSU defensive tackle Ricky-Jean François leaped high into the air to block a twenty-nine-yard field-goal attempt by Leigh Tiffin to take the game past regulation, sending 93,039 Tiger fans into a frenzy.

At halftime, the score had been knotted at 14-14 after both teams committed numerous turnovers. With six minutes remaining, LSU tailback Charles Scott tied the game at 21-21 with a one-yard plunge into the Tide end zone. LSU won the overtime coin toss, but Lee threw his fourth interception, the third pick by Alabama's Rashad Johnson. When Alabama got the ball back, quarterback John Parker Wilson threw a twenty-four-yard pass completion to Julio Jones. The signal caller then slipped into the end zone from one yard out, pushing Alabama's winning streak up to ten games and snapping the five-game winning streak that LSU held over Alabama.

Returning to Tiger Stadium for the first time since being named head coach of the

Jarrett Lee's four interceptions doomed LSU against Alabama in 2008. (Cal Sport Media via AP Images)

Tide, Saban was greeted with a resounding chorus of boos and taunted with signs reading, "Miles Over $aban." The coach later politely stated he would always have special memories of the place no matter what was said.

Although the Tigers didn't win the game, their gallant effort won the war of statistics, with 382 total yards to the Tide's 353. Lee was only thirteen of thirty-four, passing for 181 yards. Wilson wasn't much better with 215 yards, but he took much better care of the ball.

Quarterback Jordan Jefferson was on target against Alabama in 2010. (AP Photo/Bill Haber)

NUMBER 25: THE "ROLL OVER THE TIDE" GAME
LSU 24, ALABAMA 21: NOVEMBER 6, 2010

LSU coach Miles has been known to pack a bag of tricks for big games. Certainly, that was the case when number-eleven LSU upset number-five Alabama in Tiger Stadium, 24-21, in 2010. "The Mad Hatter" also tossed in two fourth-down conversions to add to the defending national champion's woes on that Saturday afternoon.

Future Heisman Trophy winner Mark Ingram and 2011 finalist Trent Richardson were kept in check by an outstanding Tiger defensive effort that held the Tide to only 102 yards rushing.

One play that totally beguiled the Tide defense was a tight-end reverse that led to a second-half point barrage, dooming Saban's return to Baton Rouge. The coach looked stunned as CBS cameras followed him jogging off the field at the end of the game.

Trailing by 1 point in the fourth quarter at the Alabama twenty-six with fourth down and one yard to go, the trickster came up with one of his best calls of the season. With the Tide defense bunched at the line of scrimmage to stop the Tiger running attack, Jordan Jefferson took the snap and quickly pitched right to running back Stevan Ridley. The tailback then handed off to tight end Deangelo Peterson, who ran the ball to the Tide three-yard line.

Ridley later rammed the ball into the end zone, giving LSU a 5 point lead. Going for 2 points, Jefferson hit Reuben Randle on a roll-out, and the Tigers had a 7-point edge. The quarterback had an outstanding afternoon, finishing ten of thirteen for 141 yards and a touchdown, while running for 27 yards on seven carries. Randle had 125 yards on only three catches. The hard-nose tailback Ridley gained 88 yards on twenty-four rushes. LSU rolled up 433 total yards to only 325 for the Tide.

On the tight-end reverse, Saban commented that if everyone had been disciplined and done what they were supposed to do in a game of that magnitude, it would not have been an issue. That might be a correct analysis of the play, but it is hardly acceptable if a call is totally unexpected. The coach could have used the same excuse in the third quarter for Josh Jasper's fake kick that resulted in a twenty-nine-yard run.

LSU would end the season 11-2, losing to Arkansas in the regular-season final and to eventual national champion Auburn, 24-17, before trouncing the Texas A&M Aggies in the seventy-fifth annual Cotton Bowl, 41-24.

NUMBER 26: THE MOST BIZARRE GAME
LSU 16, Tennessee 14: October 2, 2010

It was a game that would make anyone's head spin and that LSU had no business winning, but hey, the Tigers will take whatever someone gives them. Playing a lackluster game against an inferior Tennessee team, LSU appeared to have lost, and fans began streaming out of the stadium with consternation on their faces.

As the clock ticked down, Jefferson kept delaying the snap of the ball at the Volunteer two-yard line. A touchdown would win the game for the Tigers, but failing to get one at that point would lose it. With about eleven seconds left, players running in and out of the game, and Jefferson still not calling for the ball, center T-Bob Hebert snapped it over the head of the quarterback, who recovered it and was immediately tackled.

Booing LSU fans continued to head for the exits. But suddenly, a flag was on the field, even though there was no time left in the contest. Meanwhile, Tennessee players threw their helmets wildly into the air, celebrating the supposed victory, as LSU players threw their helmets into the turf.

After a long delay and much conferring, an official picked up the flag and announced that Tennessee had too many men on the field when the ball was snapped, resulting in a penalty. Tennessee's attempt to get new defensive players into the game while Jefferson delayed the snap had brought the flag, as play resumed when Hebert centered the ball.

Thus, the Tigers had one more chance to win the contest, at the one-yard line. And they did, as running back Stevan Ridley barreled into the end zone, carrying a Tennessee player along the way.

The hero for the Tigers was Hebert, son of former New Orleans Saints quarterback Bobby Hebert, who made the win possible by snapping the ball before time expired. The offensive lineman has probably never received proper credit for his quick thinking, but most Tiger fans know he won the game for LSU.

Ridley, who gained 132 yards on twenty-three carries and went on to star with the New England Patriots, said that it was a victory he would never forget and that some of the greatest times of his life were spent in Tiger Stadium.

NUMBER 27: THE HURRICANE GAME
TENNESSEE 30, LSU 27: SEPTEMBER 26, 2005

In their first Monday-night contest, the Tigers dropped an overtime thriller to the Volunteers, 30-27. Jumping out to a 21-0 lead in the first half on sheer emotion, the weary Tigers collapsed in the second half, allowing the Volunteers to come back and win the game. Both teams got bragging rights to the most watched college football game in the history of ESPN2, as nearly 2.8 million homes tuned in.

Hurricane Katrina had forced the Tigers to postpone their first home game against North Texas State. The second game was moved from Tiger Stadium to Arizona State, where LSU

Hurricane Katrina proved to be a detriment for LSU and quarterback JaMarcus Russell in the 2005 game against Tennessee. (AP Photo/Bill Haber)

won a dramatic contest 35-31 due to a scrambling touchdown pass from JaMarcus Russell to Early Doucet with only seconds remaining. Hurricane Rita created yet another delay for the next contest, shoving a Saturday game with the Volunteers to Monday night.

The Tigers were exhausted by the time the game began, as the LSU campus had become a recovery center for Katrina victims. Some were even housed with LSU football players.

The Tigers grabbed an early lead when quarterback Eric Ainge fumbled the ball on the Volunteers' first drive, enabling LSU to cash in with a nineteen-yard touchdown run. The score became 21-0 when Ainge threw a pass out of his end zone that was intercepted for a two-yard LSU touchdown.

The second half was a different story, however, as quarterback Rick Clausen took over for the beleaguered Ainge. The former LSU signal caller, who had transferred to Tennessee because of a lack of playing time, sneaked the ball into the end zone from one yard out, making the score 24-14 with 9:35 left in the fourth quarter.

Then Tennessee intercepted a Russell pass and returned it to the two-yard line, where Gerald Riggs ran it in for a score. The LSU crowd became quiet. With the lead down to 3 points, Tennessee forced another Tiger punt, which Riggs returned deep into LSU territory. The Volunteers then kicked another field goal, sending the game into overtime.

Winning the coin flip, the Tigers took the ball but only managed a thirty-one-yard field goal by Colt David. Riggs then accounted for Tennessee's entire yardage in overtime with a ten-yard reception and four runs. On third down, he powered into the end zone against the exhausted Tigers, winning the game for the Vols.

The Tigers, nevertheless, had an outstanding team in 2005. Their 11-2 record included a 40-3 victory over the number-ten Miami Hurricanes in the Peach Bowl in Atlanta, Georgia. The other loss was to Georgia in the SEC championship game, 34-14.

Stars representing LSU in 2005—many of whom would play in the NFL—were running back Joseph Addai, linebacker Darry Beckwith, wide receiver Dwayne Bowe, wide receiver Benny Brazell, tailback Alley Broussard, safety Jessie Daniels, wide receiver Craig Davis, defensive tackle and later All-American Glenn Dorsey, wide receiver Skyler Green, All-American defensive back LaRon Landry, offensive linemen Rudy Niswanger and Andrew Whitworth, safety Craig Steltz, and defensive tackle Claude Wroten.

NUMBER 28: THE MOST EMOTIONAL GAME
TEXAS A&M 20, LSU 18: SEPTEMBER 19, 1970

Following the outstanding 1969 season, LSU was positioned to make a run at the national championship in 1970. The previous year, the Tigers had lost only one game and had many starters back. But the Texas A&M Aggies had different ideas and shocked the Tigers in the first contest, 20-18.

Decimated by injuries and still feeling the sting of quarterback Butch Duhe's unexpected death from a brain hemorrhage, LSU lost the game with only thirteen seconds left. An A&M receiver had gotten behind the LSU defense for a seventy-nine-yard touchdown play. A silent crowd left the stadium in stunned disbelief, as the Tigers had controlled the contest most of the way.

Unbelievably, the Aggies would win no more games in 1970, while the Tigers would win the SEC championship with an array of All-Americans, especially on defense. Capturing the championship with a 9-3 record, LSU's only losses were to A&M, Notre Dame in a defensive 3-0 slugfest in South Bend, and Nebraska in the Orange Bowl, 17-12. The Bayou Bengals would finish number seven in the final AP poll. It would be McClendon's only conference title during his long tenure at LSU.

The LSU defense would be one of the greatest to suit up for the Tigers, especially on run defense. Some stars on that unit were All-American linebacker Mike Anderson, All-American tackle Ronnie Estay, All-American safety Tommy Casanova, All-SEC tackle John Sage, tackle John Wood, All-SEC safety Craig Burns, and linebacker Lloyd Frye. Notable players on offense were quarterbacks Bert Jones and Buddy Lee; Art Cantrelle, Allen Shorey, and Chris Dantin at running back; and Andy Hamilton and Gerald Keigley at wide receiver.

Joseph Addai led LSU to a huge upset win over Auburn in 2005. (AP Photo/Michael Conroy)

NUMBER 29: "THE NIGHT THE KICKER CHOKED" GAME
LSU 20, Auburn 17: October 22, 2005

Auburn's John Vaughn went from hero to goat after missing five straight field-goal attempts in a game that the War Eagles should have won if not for his ineptitude. He was a hero earlier in an Auburn win but had the tables turned on him in Death Valley. After making a twenty-six-yard field goal in the second quarter, Vaughn regressed, missing the potential game winner at the end of the contest.

Tied at 17 at the end of regulation, Auburn won the coin toss and chose to defend. LSU kicker Chris Jackson made a thirty-yard attempt on the Tigers' first possession in overtime. Up next, Auburn made only two yards with its possession and sent out Vaughn again in an attempt to knot the score. As the ball hit the left upright and fell away from the crossbars, 92,664 LSU fans—a record for that time—wildly celebrated the 20-17 victory.

Auburn won the statistical war but lost the game because of the missed field goals. Kenny Irons rushed for 221 yards on twenty-seven carries, as LSU failed to slow down Auburn's running game. Auburn also led in total yards, 451 to the Tigers' 329. The War Eagles had won thirteen straight SEC games until this bitter loss.

LSU's Joseph Addai ran for 105 yards in the Tigers' fourth straight victory that season.

Archie Manning was a thorn in LSU's side in a wild 1968 contest. (AP Photo)

NUMBER 30: THE "SUPERMAN TAKES CHARGE" GAME
OLE MISS 27, LSU 24: SEPTEMBER 19, 1968

In a great offensive showdown in 1968, Archie Manning rallied Ole Miss to a heart-pounding 27-24 win over LSU in the last three minutes of the game. The Tigers had triumphed in a 1964 contest against the Rebels in Baton Rouge when a tipped ball was caught in the end zone for a 2-point conversion. With that loss still on its radar, Mississippi turned the tables on the Tigers when a tipped ball was caught in the LSU end zone by an Ole Miss receiver who was falling backward.

At 5-1, LSU was facing future All-American Archie Manning for the first time. The Drew, Mississippi, native was not only a great passer but also a tremendous runner who baffled defenders with his quick moves and speed during his three-year tenure with the Rebels. Looking as though he had stepped right out of the Superman comic books, the quarterback dazzled an overflow crowd of nearly seventy thousand fans in Tiger Stadium by completing twenty-four passes for 345 yards against a stingy LSU defense. Coach Vaught had decided to give Manning free rein, believing that the sophomore signal caller could be the all-time best at Mississippi, even ranking over Jack Gibbs, Bobby Franklin, and others.

Mike Hillman came off the bench for LSU, replacing quarterback Freddy Haynes, who suffered a dislocated wrist in the first quarter. The Tigers took an early 17-3 lead in the contest and seemingly had the Rebels where they wanted them. However, Manning was able to connect on a sixty-five-yard pass play to Floyd Franks for a touchdown. Then an interception by Ole Miss set up another touchdown, and suddenly the game was tied at 17-17.

With time running out, LSU's Don Addison took the ball away from a Rebel receiver and the Tigers kicked a field goal, taking a 24-20 lead with just three minutes left in the game. Many spectators thought the Tigers had control of the contest, but they were wrong, and the offensive slugfest went down to the wire. Managing the clock to perfection, Manning fought his way down the field with precision passing and stuck a knife in the heart of the Tigers with a 3-point win.

The Tigers won the stat sheet against Ole Miss, gaining 458 yards to the Rebels' 454. But as in 1961, the final score was the only thing that counted when the horn sounded to end the contest. LSU would finish the season 8-3 and defeat Florida State in the inaugural Peach Bowl, 31-27.

Tigers on the roster that would make headlines were receivers Tommy Morel and Bill Stober, tailback Maurice LeBlanc, quarterback Mike Hillman, defensive tackle John Sage, fullback and placekicker Eddie Ray, tackle Bill Fortier, running back Kenny Newfield, linebacker Bill Thomason, and defensive back Craig Burns.

HONORABLE MENTIONS

So there you have it—the thirty greatest games ever played in Tiger Stadium. Let the debates begin.

Many more memorable games have been played in Tiger Stadium since the 1950s. A few deserve honorable mentions.

In a 1979 contest, top-ranked Alabama slipped past LSU, 3-0. The game might have made my top thirty if it had not been played in a driving rainstorm, which slowed both teams down. Alabama rushed for 252 yards while holding the Tigers to only 164. LSU quarterback Steve Ensminger was intercepted twice. The only score in the game was Alan McElroy's field goal in the third quarter.

On its road to the national championship in 1958, LSU defeated Ole Miss, 14-0, in a game that was closer than the score. In the first half, the Rebels drove deep into Tiger territory but were stopped four times at the Bengal one-foot line. Mississippi was a 3-point favorite, despite the fact that the Tigers were ranked number one in the nation. Quarterbacks Warren Rabb and Durel Mathern were offensive stars in this contest, in which LSU once again flexed its defensive muscle.

In 2006, Auburn won the "Grand Theft" game, 7-3, in one of the most physical matchups between these two teams. LSU wide receiver Early Doucet was clearly interfered with on a fourth-down play with three minutes left. But to the dismay of Bengal fans, a referee picked up the flag. With a final chance to win, Russell floated a pass to Craig Davis near the Auburn end zone, but it was knocked down by a War Eagle defender. LSU filed a complaint with the SEC against the officiating crew but to no avail.

In a 2002 contest, quarterback Marcus Randall came off the bench to rally LSU past Ole Miss, 14-13. He completed thirteen of twenty passes for 179 yards and two touchdowns. Behind 6 points with 6:34 remaining in the game, Randall hit Michael Clayton for a 29-yard touchdown pass, overtaking the Rebels by 1 point. Five fumbles by LSU, three of which were lost, kept Ole Miss alive. Although the Tiger offense struggled, the defense limited Mississippi to 61 yards rushing. Ole Miss quarterback Eli Manning was sacked twice and intercepted twice.

In a 1997 offensive duel in which neither team could stop the other, Auburn outlasted LSU, 31-

Cecil Collins was an outstanding running back at LSU in 1997. (AP Photo/NFL Photos)

28. The Tigers' Cecil Collins ran for 232 yards on twenty-seven carries, while Rondell Mealey had 120 yards on just twelve carries. However, Auburn's Dameyune Craig passed for over 300 yards. With a short run up the middle for a touchdown, the War Eagles won the game with only seconds remaining on the clock.

In 1986, the Tigers won the SEC title but lost to Ole Miss at home, 21-19, when LSU kicker David Browndyke missed a field goal from thirty yards out with nine seconds left to play. Behind 21-9 at halftime, LSU came back on the arm of quarterback Tommy Hodson and the receiving of All-American Wendell Davis but fell short by 2 points. Nevertheless, LSU had a great season with a victory over Notre Dame, 21-19, and Alabama, 14-10, in Birmingham. Unfortunately, the Tigers lost to Nebraska in the Sugar Bowl, 30-15. Head Coach Bill Arnsparger would return to Florida in 1987 after a successful three-year tenure in Tigertown.

The LSU-Arkansas matchup in 2007 was clearly a great contest. It has been relegated to an honorable mention here, because the game faded from view after the Tigers won the BCS National Championship in New Orleans that same season. Darren McFadden rushed for 206 yards and three touchdowns and passed for another, leading Arkansas to a 50-48 win over the number-one Tigers in triple overtime. The LSU defense had several key injuries that contributed to the loss.

LSU got an extra dose of incentive for this barnburner in 1995 as the Tigers donned their white jerseys at home for the first time in fifteen years. In a campaign to "bring back the magic" to a team that had had several losing seasons in a row, new head coach Gerry DiNardo and unranked LSU stung number-five Auburn, 12-6, in a stunning SEC upset. *Sporting News* said the Tiger crowd was so loud for this contest that Auburn quarterback Patrick Nix, standing in his end zone in the first quarter, mistakenly thought he heard a whistle blow. Tackling him in the end zone, LSU tacked on a 2-point conversion and went on to win the game.

In a 2001 game postponed by the September 11 terrorist attacks, LSU defeated Auburn, 27-14, on December 1. Auburn riled Tiger fans and players before the start of the game by jumping on the Eye of the Tiger at midfield, while Tommy Tuberville smoked a cigar. Kicking from the five-yard line after a fifteen-yard penalty, LSU recovered an onside kick and matched to an early touchdown. The Tigers clinched a berth in the SEC championship game with the victory over Auburn.

Wide receiver Brandon LaFell high steps into the end zone against Middle Tennessee State in 2007. (AP Photo/ Alex Brandon)

CHAPTER THREE

THE ASCENSION OF LSU FOOTBALL

Since the beginning of the new century, LSU has become one of the most prominent college football teams in the nation, hanging two more national championship banners in Tiger Stadium. But it was not always that way for the Bayou Bengals.

Just a few years before—for a large portion of the 1990s—LSU was an afterthought in the minds of many college football fans. The Purple and Gold had lost its reputation as one of the tougher teams in the nation. The Tigers reeled off several losing seasons, and recruiting was makeshift. Many of the best players from the New Orleans area went to more successful schools.

A glance at the history of the Tigers reveals that fanatical devotion to LSU football began in 1958. Due to a crop of local talent that year, the Purple and Gold won its first national title, seemingly out of nowhere. As game attendance soared, the fervor moved into 1959 with Head Coach Paul Dietzel leading the charge.

On Halloween night in 1959, LSU defeated Ole Miss, 7-3, in a game between two defensive titans, and suddenly LSU and Tiger Stadium appeared on the national radar. Billy Cannon's astonishing eighty-nine-yard touchdown run over and through more than half of the Rebel football team ramped up the attention. The Bayou Bengals were off and running, with a nineteen-game winning streak in the record books. Only a loss to Tennessee in Knoxville marred the 1959 regular season.

The winning ways continued into the early 1960s, as Dietzel produced one of LSU's greatest teams in 1961 with an SEC championship and an undefeated conference run. A lone loss to Rice after the Tigers committed several costly turnovers in the initial game possibly left LSU out of national championship contention. When Dietzel departed for Army, defensive coach Charles McClendon filled the void.

In 1962, the wins continued for the Tigers, as LSU ripped its way to a 9-1-1 season and a 13-0 victory over undefeated Texas in the Cotton Bowl. Only a 15-7 loss to Ole Miss and a 6-6 tie with Rice marred the year. Running back Jerry Stovall finished second in the Heisman Trophy voting, but this team won games mostly with its trademark defense.

From 1963 to 1968, McClendon's teams slipped somewhat into mediocrity, with several three- and four-loss seasons. Then in 1969, LSU fielded one of its greatest contingents with a single defeat, 26-23 to Ole Miss in Oxford, which could have gone either way. Thus, it was another close miss for the national championship trophy.

The 1970s brought more three- and four-loss seasons. However, 1970 was a banner year with an SEC championship, and the Tigers continued to have one of the top defensive units in the nation. McClendon came under fire when 1974-75 failed to produce winning records, and the longtime LSU coach was finally forced out in 1979.

The College Football Hall of Fame mentor finished his eighteen-year career at LSU with a glittering 137-59-7 winning mark. But he had failed to get the Tigers over the hump against Alabama or win a national championship. Also, in the eyes of some football fans, McClendon had become expendable because of his view of passing only out of necessity. An exception

Charlie McClendon posted a glittering 137-59-7 record for LSU. (AP Photo)

occurred in 1969, when he fielded one of LSU's most balanced attacks.

After McClendon's dismissal, the Tigers began a slow, downward slide that didn't end until the next century. A few good seasons were mixed in with a lot of poor and mediocre ones.

Former running back great Jerry Stovall took the helm at LSU from 1980to 1983, after new head coach Robert "Bo" Rein, before ever taking the field, was tragically killed in a plane crash. Stovall led the Tigers to the Orange Bowl during an outstanding 8-3-1 campaign in 1982. However, after failing to win a single conference game in 1983, he was shown the door.

Bill Arnsparger, a highly respected NFL defensive coach in the 1970s, had success at LSU during a short tenure from 1984 to 1986. His victories included an SEC title along with a 14-10 whipping of Alabama in Birmingham, a game that wasn't as close as the score.

Defensive coordinator Mike Archer took over from 1987 to 1990 and had one brilliant season in 1987, when the Tigers went 10-1-1 and captured the SEC championship. Finishing with a number-five ranking, LSU lost only to Alabama, 22-10, and had a 10-10 tie with Ohio State. The injury of Tommy Hodson, who was held out for the Tide game, probably resulted in the lone loss for the Tigers and kept them from having a shot at the national championship. However, after losing seasons in 1989 and 1990, Archer was fired.

The 1990s were the darkest years for the Tigers, as questionable coaching and a lack of productive recruiting resulted mostly in mediocre to bad teams. Curley Hallman, hired from Southern Mississippi after Archer was fired in 1990, had four straight losing seasons from 1991 to 1994. The 1992 season netted only two victories.

However, Hallman does have the distinction of pulling off one of the most mind-boggling upsets in college football with a 17-13 win over Alabama in Tuscaloosa. The 1993 victory ended the Tide's thirty-one-game winning streak under Coach Gene Stallings. Nevertheless, that same season—LSU's centennial year—the Tigers lost to Florida at home, 58-3, the worse defeat in school history. The following year, "the giant killer" coached his last game at LSU. He had earned the moniker at Southern Mississippi by defeating Alabama and other prominent college football teams.

Next came Gerry DiNardo, who promised to "bring back the magic" to LSU football. In his first three campaigns, the former Notre Dame lineman did wave his magic wand and led the Tigers to winning records and three post-season contests, including the 1996 Peach Bowl, in which the Tigers finished with a sparkling 10-2 mark. However, during the 1998-99 seasons, LSU won only seven games, and DiNardo was fired.

Finally the worm turned for the Purple and Gold when LSU hired Nick Saban from Michigan State in 2000. Recruiting some of the most talented players in the land, Saban started winning almost immediately, instilling confidence in a downtrodden program. The 1990s—a decade in which the Tigers had seven losing seasons and a record of 54-58-1—were finally over for LSU.

Through coaching hires and outstanding recruiting, the Tigers became a football powerhouse once again. Most deserving of the Bayou Bengals' big leap into the highest echelons of college football, however, were undoubtedly the fans. Nowhere in America can you find a more diehard and fanatical following of a football team. To the fans of the Purple and Gold, LSU football is a

Gerry DiNardo brought back the magic to LSU for three seasons. (AP Photo/Dave Martin)

religion of life and death, talked about year round. Weddings rarely occur on Saturdays when LSU is playing in Tiger Stadium.

After the surprising year in 1958, LSU fans' forty-five-year wait finally paid off. From 2003 to 2007, LSU won two national championships and was the toast of the college football world. Saban grabbed the first championship in 2003 before heading to the Miami Dolphins and eventually Alabama. In 2007, LSU won its third national championship, led by Les Miles, "The Mad Hatter." The climb back into national prominence had been accomplished, and it continued into 2011 with an SEC championship and 2012 with another winning campaign.

A lot of credit for the Bayou Bengals' continued success after Saban departed should go to Miles, hired in 2005 from Oklahoma State. While at LSU, the coach twice declined to coach his alma mater, Michigan, even though that's where he had played as an offensive lineman, met his wife, and served as assistant coach. Miles knew what side his bread was buttered on, and that was LSU, where he could recruit some of the best players in the land.

Miles also brought aboard a brilliant defensive coordinator in John Chavis from Tennessee, who molded some of the quickest and hardest-hitting defenses in the nation. It also should be noted that Miles, a former college player himself, related to his teams in a special way that gained respect, attention, and—most important—love. Both a successful recruiter and coach, with just a few possible game exceptions, Miles was accepted by the players as being "one of them."

In 2011, LSU made one of its greatest runs with Miles at the helm. Pummeling thirteen straight opponents, including three that were ranked in the top five, LSU made its way to the conference title and a 13-1 mark. A 21-0 loss to Alabama in the BCS National Championship game in New Orleans—in which LSU inexplicably played its worst game of the season—ended the Tigers' winning streak. LSU had defeated Alabama 9-6 earlier in the season at Tuscaloosa but looked as though it were sleepwalking in the championship contest, as the offense failed to sustain any momentum.

College football history has suggested that a team losing the first game has a big psychological edge in a rematch, especially if the teams are evenly matched. Look no further than LSU football itself. In 1997, the Bayou Bengals were overwhelmed in a regular-season loss to Notre Dame at Tiger Stadium, 24-6. In a rematch at the Independence Bowl, the Tigers turned the tables on the Fighting Irish, 27-9. And in 1959, LSU defeated Ole Miss 7-3 in the regular season but lost to the Rebels in the Sugar Bowl, 21-0.

But give kudos to the Tide, because LSU was not as prepared as Alabama for the national championship contest. LSU coaches must have believed that the Tide would rely on its running game with Trent Richardson, as in the first game. Instead, the Red Elephant came out passing, throwing the Tiger defense off stride. On defense, Alabama stacked the line of scrimmage, totally stuffing the LSU running attack. Jordan Jefferson was unsure of himself the entire game and rarely had time to set up, as the Tide brought heavy pressure from all angles.

It has been easy for many fans to write off this season because of the one loss at the end of the year. Instead, Bengal fans should view it as one of the Tigers' greatest years. LSU beat a tremendous team on its own turf. Why were the Tigers asked to do it once more in New Orleans? That was the question that went unanswered. The team that lost the first game would instinctively be more motivated in the rematch, even though LSU players and coaches would probably never admit or even be conscious of that.

And so Alabama was crowned the national champion after failing to win the Southeastern

LSU running back Jeremy Hill breaks loose for a touchdown against South Carolina in 2012. (AP Photo/ Gerald Herbert)

Miles has recruited some of the best players in the nation for LSU. (AP Photo/Stephen Morton, File)

Conference or even the West Division. Shame should follow the BCS voters that year for overlooking Oklahoma State, which had more top-twenty-five victories than the Tide. Sure, the Cowboys had one bad loss to Iowa State, but why penalize the team, especially after the tragedy with the women's basketball squad occurring around the same time? The controversial BCS system might be improved by the new playoff system set to begin in 2014. However, fans and players must remember that no system is perfect and arguments will continue. Even so, the fiasco of 2012 probably won't recur.

An accurate assessment of the 2011 team shows that the Tigers didn't have multiple media stars, concerned about individual statistics. Instead, LSU played with great cohesion the entire regular season, with third stringers sometimes outshining first stringers. No one or two players carried the load and received all the hype—everyone did his job, resulting in one of the greatest LSU football teams.

Through one of the most difficult schedules a team could face, the Bayou Bengals won a record thirteen games in a season. Carrying LSU to the title game were outstanding special teams, a formidable defense with great speed, and a punter who could get the Tigers out of a hole or push the opponent into one. Another element that made this team very productive was its ability to overcome tough obstacles. When Offensive Coordinator Steve Kragthorpe was discovered to have Parkinson's, without missing a beat the Tigers switched him to quarterback coach, a position with fewer duties, and made Greg Strudawa the offensive coordinator.

For the several games in which starters were out because of injuries or suspensions, backups played just as well or even better, and the winning streak continued. When quarterback Jefferson and linebacker Joshua Johns were suspended for several games on battery charges, the Tigers pounded eight straight teams—including some highly ranked ones—under the leadership and superb play of quarterback Lee. When Miles suspended three Tiger players—Mathieu, tailback Spencer Ware, and defensive back Tharold Simon—from the Auburn game for violating team rules, LSU nonetheless crushed Auburn, 45-10. From the start of the season, team chemistry and depth made this contingent outstanding. If defensive end Barkevious Mingo or All-American Sam Montgomery weren't slamming a quarterback into the turf, wide receiver Rueben Randle was hauling in a touchdown pass from Jefferson or Lee; or Bennie Logan and Josh Downs were stuffing a running back at the line of scrimmage; or "The Honey Badger" was taking a ball away from a receiver or scoring on a kickoff; or All-American defensive back Mo Claiborne was intercepting a ball and running it back for a touchdown; or offensive linemen P. J. Lonergan and All-American Will Blackwell were making big holes for running backs; or Brad Wing was punting a ball seventy yards in the air to get the Tigers into a better field position.

Few teams can accomplish the following in one season, but LSU did: defeated number-three Oregon, 40-27, at neutral Dallas; won at number-twenty-five Mississippi State, 19-6; won at number-sixteen West Virginia, 47-21; crushed number-seventeen Florida, 41-17, at home; blasted number-nineteen Auburn in Tiger Stadium, 45-10; upset number-two Alabama, 9-6, in Tuscaloosa; crushed number-three Arkansas, 41-17, at home; and then humbled the Georgia Bulldogs, 42-10, in Atlanta for the SEC championship. Before the season was over, the Tigers tallied five AP All-Americans—defensive backs Claiborne and Mathieu, punter Wing, offensive guard Blackwell, and defensive end Montgomery.

With the big disappointment in New Orleans behind them, things were looking up for the Tigers in the 2012 season, as many pollsters tabbed them number one in preseason balloting. But as fate would have it, star player and Heisman Trophy finalist Mathieu was kicked off the

Rueben Randle catches a touchdown pass against Western Kentucky in 2011.
(Cal Sport Media via AP Images)

Michael Ford runs for forty-nine yards in a win against Arkansas in 2011. (AP Photo/Gerald Herbert)

team before the season began for allegedly failing several drug tests. Losing "The Honey Badger," who had a knack for stealing the ball away from opponents and scoring touchdowns, was a great blow to the Tigers.

With Mathieu on the team, LSU would have probably defeated Alabama at home in 2012 and possibly Florida, too. A national championship might have been in the offing, but Miles should be credited for dismissing the troubled star when he reportedly failed to observe team rules. No one player, whether a star or not, can break team rules and expect to remain on the squad if the coach has any integrity. Certainly Miles does.

But LSU moved on. In 2013, it had a top-five recruiting class and looked to have the number-one class in 2014. It appears LSU will stay near the top of the college football world for a very, very long time to come, and Tiger Stadium will maintain its reputation for ferocity for many decades into the future.

Jarvis Landry makes a spectacular catch against Arkansas in 2012. (AP Photo/David Quinn)

AFTERWORD

The author will always remember Tiger Stadium as a place where chills run up and down the body when the band marches out. Even a memory of LSU football and Tiger Stadium is enough to make one's skin tingle with excitement. There's no place in college football that stirs the emotions or has the magic of Tiger Stadium. It's a high that one doesn't forget and makes the senses come alive in a special way that's hard to duplicate. The energy and emotions of Tiger fans are stirred to a fever pitch during night games, resulting in one of the loudest and scariest venues in the entire world!